JONAH BONDI WISE

JONAH BONDI WISE

A BIOGRAPHY BY

SAM CAUMAN

CROWN PUBLISHERS · NEW YORK

Library of Congress Catalog Card Number: 66–29745
Printed and bound in Japan

Contents

Introduction

In America, in Israel, and in many other lands, there are countless thousands whose very lives are a memorial to Rabbi B. Wise's initiative, energy, and courage. The present generation can hardly realize what it meant for this man to walk into the land of the Hitler horror, to gather the oppressed, the disillusioned, and the bewildered, to comfort them and put them back on the road to truly human existence. Comparatively few among those saved were aware of how much they owed him, for he was a member of a team, nay, an army, and never dramatized himself or his role of leader. Even so, for weeks after his death the Central Synagogue phone would ring from time to time and a voice at the other end of the line would say, "If it were not for Jonah Wise, I wouldn't be here." Letters of appreciation came from little, obscure people and from important, prominent people who had been enabled through him to repair their shattered lives and live in dignity and hope.

The seven years since we lost Rabbi Wise are a short time in which to see his service to the helpless and oppressed in proper historical perspective. Yet I believe that this biography has accomplished that purpose—and I am grateful to the author for beginning and ending it with verses from the 29th chapter of the *Book of Job*: "Because I delivered the poor that cried...."

I myself was a younger colleague of Rabbi Wise. It took me some time to get to know him. He had a gruff and sometimes hard exterior. He was sharp of wit and quick of tongue; and his sense of humor was sometimes like a rapier. Some people thought you just couldn't reach him. But when I underwent a major operation and my wife left her children to keep vigil at the hospital, Rabbi Wise came to my house and sat with my two little girls. That grand, formidable gentleman had a way with children, and he was able to comfort them in that difficult moment. Beneath his protective armor he was tender, understanding, and completely human.

Other younger colleagues, the sons of Orthodox immigrants, remember with deep gratitude how he befriended them, personally encouraged them, tutored them for admission to Hebrew Union College, and inspired them in their Ministry. Jonah Wise was uncompromising in his conviction of the validity of the Reform interpretation of Judaism, but his interest in and service to Jews of every description was wholehearted.

He was a unique personality in the American Rabbinate, but he was also a faithful follower of a great tradition; like his sainted father, he believed that America, a land of hope and freedom for all men, was a natural home for our ancient faith and its message of world redemption. In our day, we see increasingly the fulfillment of his vision of the future of American Jews. It is my hope that the readers of this volume will recognize, as Jonah Wise did, the essential harmony of Judaism and Americanism as they and their children walk in dignity as equal citizens of our great democracy.

David J. Seligson

Preface

THE PUBLIC LIFE OF JONAH BONDI WISE is, largely, a matter of record. His private life is something else again. He kept it private, which is something that no rabbi can do without a major effort, and (if I have read his character correctly) had no desire to expose it to uninvited guests. A piously sentimental or obsequiously flattering literary monument to his memory would have annoyed him—and, indeed, such tenderness does not pay respect to the subject of a biography, for it signifies that he was scarcely good enough to be put down just as he was. Rabbi Wise did not have to be told these things; he knew them. Accordingly, he would have taken a hard look at the proposal that some stranger write a book about him. I have not written for him, however, but for a congregation that loved and admired him and for a people whom he sustained in a time of great extremity. They have much to remember him for, yet, without some token of remembrance, men easily slip into forgetfulness of the dead. Hence this book. But it is my hope that Rabbi Wise would feel no embarrassment if he could read these pages, and would recognize himself in this portrait.

S. C.

JONAH BONDI WISE

The Background

AT EVERY IMPORTANT MILESTONE in his career, Jonah Bondi Wise found himself sharing the platform and applause with the memory of his father, Isaac Mayer Wise; and it is not inappropriate that he should do so again in the first chapters of this book. The younger Wise was a man to remember, the elder a man not to be forgotten; between them, over a background of a century and more, they made an outstanding contribution to Judaism, to the Jewish people, and to America. Isaac Mayer Wise made America the world center of Reform Judaism; he was a tireless innovator and organizer. Jonah Bondi Wise helped bring American Reform Judaism to its full flowering and, for the last twenty-five years of his life, performed a shining service in the immense task of saving Europe's Jews from Hitler's murder camps. Both men played a central role in the integration of Jews into organized American life and in the establishment of the identity of Jews as members of one of the three recognized major American religious bodies.

Reform Judaism and Isaac Mayer Wise were both prod-
ucts of the Enlightenment. The Enlightenment, originating in England with the philosophy of John Locke and
deriving from the scientific revolution of the seventeenth
century, was the dominant intellectual faith of the eighteenth. Human reason, it was believed, could render the
entire universe intelligible. The rational condition for
human relations was regarded as freedom, equality, and
opportunity for all. Translated into political action through
the energies of the American and French revolutions, the
Enlightenment eventually gave full citizenship to Jews—
hitherto excluded from participating in civil life. Jewish
emancipation marched with Napoleon's armies, and, by
1800, had been extended to the western states of Germany.

Jews participated early in the German Enlightenment.
In the middle of the eighteenth century, the gentile philosopher Lessing proposed the thesis, utterly astonishing to
the Germans of his day, that Jews were capable of nobility
of spirit. His real-life example was Moses Mendelssohn of
Dessau, the model for his literary hero in *Nathan the Wise*.
Mendelssohn advocated the abandonment of the Jewish
folk language, Yiddish (medieval German fused with Hebrew and written in Hebrew characters), in favor of the national language, German. He turned from Bible and Talmud study to the secular philosophy of the Enlightenment.
"I recognize no eternal verities," he declared in his *Jerusalem*, "except those which can not only be conceived but also
be established and verified by human reason."[1] This was a
crucial turning that ruptured the sheltering cocoon of Jewish existence. Thereafter—for Mendelssohn had many followers—educated Jews in Germany's metropolitan centers

---

[1]Quoted by Isidore Epstein in *Judaism*, p. 287.

were to be modern in spirit and oriented toward the entire sweep of the modern world. Laws, ceremonies, ideas, and institutions that had guided the Jews for centuries during their ghetto existence now tumbled as emancipation became a rapid current that merged with the mainstream of Western civilization. As Jews emerged from the protective seclusion of their own life and institutions, they inevitably experienced a crisis of faith and identity. What, now, was a Jew? Where were his loyalties?[2]

When it is possible to fit new events into patterns carrying over from the past, we accept everything that we are given, new or old. We are not presented with any problems and there is no need to open ourselves to change. But when we cannot fit the new events into the old schemes, we feel displaced and uncertain; we are compelled to shift ground. Perhaps it is possible to retire from the challenge altogether and shrink back, rejecting everything new, burrowing into the refuge of the past and letting the world go by. This is a destructive outcome—to the extent, at least, of settling for a less creative equilibrium with society and events than would have been possible otherwise. During the days of the emancipation, to have kept old religious and social forms—so narrow, so exclusive, so medieval, so barren, with so little bearing on actual life—would have been deliberate regression. For, given courage enough and the creative ability to reshape key institutions and keep life

---

[2]Astonishingly enough—for Jewish studies are beyond all doubt a conspicuously neglected realm of modern scholarship, being generally regarded as belonging to religious history alone—we are today no nearer answers to these questions than we were at the dawn of the emancipation two centuries and a quarter ago. It is not within the province of this book to come to grips with the issues involved, which divide all Jews, professing or otherwise. Not race, not "nationality," not religion seems to be the key. In 1966, as in 1766, each Jew finds his own answer.

organized as change takes place, we can broaden the horizons of a faith, retaining from the traditional past what is fundamental and enduring, abandoning what is superficial and nonessential. The reformist Jews in Germany had this courage and creative ability in ample measure, adhering to the prophetic and universal aspects of their religion as they stripped away an incrustation of tribal taboos and formalized ceremonies, now drained of significance. There were casualties in this operation—as in any where risks are taken —and a number of "Germans of the Mosaic persuasion" ceased to be persuaded, joining one or another of the Christian churches. In spite of these changes of heart, Reform Judaism was born in Germany in the opening years of the nineteenth century. Its highest development took place in America, after being carried there by emigrants who did not wish to live under the political and social reaction that followed the Congress of Vienna.

A "temple" was built at Seesen, near Brunswick, in 1810. There, boys were confirmed collectively at Pentecost rather than individually on the Sabbath nearest their thirteenth birthday. Torah reading at congregational services was abandoned. Sermons were delivered in German. Hymns and prayers were rendered in German as well as in Hebrew, to the accompaniment of the organ.

Some of these innovations were, no doubt, superficial; but let us take a good look at some of the others. For example, the denotation of a house of worship by the name "temple" is of the utmost significance. Inherent in this choice of words is the rejection of the whole medieval tradition of rabbinism, in which—after the destruction of the Temple in Jerusalem—the center of worship was the meeting house, or "synagogue." The reference to the Temple

also signifies a return to the bedrock of prerabbinic Judaism, disentangled from the jungle growths of nearly seventeen hundred years. Again, the destruction of the Temple
in the first century marked the beginning of the Exile,
in which Jews wandered over the earth as strangers and
aliens, and were to wander until the Messiah would redeem
them and restore them to their own land. Thus, choosing
the name "temple" also signified the re-edification of the
Temple and the ending of the Exile. Now the Jews were
being redeemed, the Messiah, in this case, being the Jewish
community itself, through its own efforts, in Germany, not
in the Land of Zion. Or, rather, Germany was taking the
place of the Land of Zion. Take the organ. Use of the organ
was by no means an innocuous innovation intended only to
enrich the liturgy. Musical instruments had been used in
the service of the Temple in ancient Jerusalem; and, after
the Destruction, their use had been proscribed until the
Temple would exist once more and the Jews, accordingly,
would no longer be in exile. The Seesen temple's organ
strains, therefore, proclaimed that Jews were Germans
worshiping their God in their homeland.

East of the Vistula, integration of the Jews into general
society became a movement that affected only the small
number who lived in the great cities. Even these did not
carry the process too far forward, and were "Jews in the
home and men in the street." They lived in an almost completely nonaccepting gentile environment, and only by the
most heroic efforts of optimistic self-deception could they
have convinced themselves that they were no longer living
in exile. Eighty per cent of Europe's Jews lived in the East—
some three million souls. Almost all of this great number
lived in tiny villages, unaffected by the great transforming

events of the eighteenth and nineteenth centuries and separated from the expanding modern world by space as well as by time. They remained a civilization within a civilization—Jews, not Russians; Jews, not Poles; Jews, not Romanians. They were a people with an intense inner life centered on the Bible and the Talmud and averted from a violently hostile non-Jewish world. In that ghetto world, the Renaissance and the Enlightenment had not yet displaced the Middle Ages. The world outside men's heads was full of hidden meanings whose unraveling revealed God's plans for creation. The Eastern Jews, like Orthodox Jews the world over, lived in accordance with the *shulchan aruch*, the extraordinary sixteenth-century legalistic code of Joseph Caro. This highly elaborate set of regulations guided every act of a Jewish person from dawn till midnight and from the cradle to the grave. Its rules were so special as to wall the Jews away from the rest of the world. The rigors of its dos and don'ts were a straitjacket on life and thought, an expression of utter hopelessness of ever finding a place for Jews beside the rest of mankind. Nevertheless, this self-imposed discipline was an amazing demonstration, unique in history, of a people's ability to shrink in upon itself and survive the most crushing persecution. Accustomed to finding scriptural inspiration, this Bible-centered folk took to heart the admonition of the prophet Isaiah:

Go, my people. Flee into thy inner chamber. Close the door after you, till the storm shall pass.

The first workings of emancipation in Eastern Europe came a century later than in Germany, and then not in a form marked by acceptance of the institutions of the ruling groups. Its major intellectual and cultural vehicles, rather than religious reform, were revolutionary socialism, political Zionism, and, to some extent, rejection of religion. Many differences in attitude between Jews with Reform and Jews with Orthodox backgrounds stem from a split development, and, with numerous ramifications, remain with us today.

Emancipation found harder going in the Empire of Austria-Hungary than in the western states of the German Confederation. The Emperor Joseph II encouraged integration of the Jews, and, in his Edict of Toleration, 1781, invited them to adopt the German language and to open schools for secular education. In the early nineteenth century, however, conditions for the Jews returned to the levels that had existed for centuries. Except in the minds of a few men, the liberation following the French Revolution never reached the eastern fastnesses of Austria, Bohemia, Hungary, or the South Slavic lands. There, the Jews were not citizens and had no rights; they lived on sufferance. A Jew might manage every *pfennig* for a great landholding noble, but could not himself own land or work on it. He could be a moneylender, an artisan, or a small shopkeeper, but other occupations were proscribed.

In every way, not just in its treatment of Jews, the Austrian Empire of Emperor Ferdinand I, Prince Metternich—and Rabbi Isaac Mayer Wise—was a vast prison, the prototype of the modern police state. Metternich was supreme in international affairs. He was the architect of the short-lived Austro-Prussian-Russian Holy Alliance, to which every Continental country attached itself. The Holy Alliance, in the name of stability, sought to turn back the clock of history and the memory of popular freedoms under

Napoleon's proconsuls. Its immediate intentions were to suppress all national or popular movements—without fail in Europe, but, if possible, anywhere else in the world as well. Metternich was dedicated to the revival and perpetuation of monarchic absolutism, religious establishment, economic monopoly, and aristocratic privilege. He hated and feared the young republic of the United States of America as a world focus of democratic infection. A beacon to malcontents and subversives, the United States had come into being through revolution; and its sustained existence was a threat to the stability of monarchies everywhere. President Monroe's recently promulgated doctrine had exhibited the effrontery of limiting the Holy Alliance's sphere of action to the Old World and of encouraging republican rebellions in the American colonies of the ancient monarchy of Spain. Yet Metternich was a wide-eyed liberal by comparison with Ferdinand's father, the Emperor Francis I. The rigidity of Francis' internal policies was too much for him, and he constantly and unsuccessfully strove to mitigate them.

Francis I was supreme in the internal affairs of his multinational empire, and his son Ferdinand carried on his policies unchanged. Francis' chief deputy was Count Sedlnitzki, commissioner of police. No effective opposition was possible to Sedlnitzki's brutally oppressive rule. His spies, paid and unpaid, were everywhere, making daily checks on persons of consequence and opening every letter sent by public post. Schools and universities were minutely scrutinized and disciplined to maintain conformity with ultraconservative ideas. Iron censorship was clamped on writers and publishers. All speeches at public meetings were carefully recorded and reported to Sedlnitzki's officials.

The Europe he knew, gripped by antisemitism and post-Napoleonic political reaction, was a poisonous area to Isaac Mayer Wise. He saw no future there for Jews or Judaism. "I had a mother tongue—German," he used to say grimly. His mother had been allowed to speak to her children in the language of the country. His father, he would go on to say, had not been allowed to call a hairsbreadth of land his own. "Therefore, I never had a fatherland."[3]

In Radnice, Bohemia, in 1845, Isaac Mayer Wise performed a marriage ceremony over a betrothed couple. We know next to nothing about this pair—only that they wanted to marry and that Wise was willing to risk major trouble in order to uphold their right to do so. His act of marrying them was proper to his rabbinical calling, but did get him into major trouble for violating the law of *Familienrecht*—the quota of Jewish families in the district was already full. Not only were the administrative authorities furious, but so were the leaders of the Jewish community, who had no disposition to challenge their masters. Wise was by no means the rabbi Radnice wanted. He was not a man to let sleeping dogs lie. He had felt the breath of the Enlightenment, received a secular education (because of his

---

[3]Heine (as Herbert Agar noted in *The Saving Remnant*, his account of the role of the JDC in Jewish survival) "divined all the tragedy of the German Jew." In his ironic poem *Es war ein Traum*, the great German-Jewish poet touched on the psychological predicament of nineteenth-century emancipated Jews, who dropped their ancient defenses and wooed their German homeland and its life and culture with the most ardent and yearning patriotism, only to encounter scornful rejection:

Ich hatte einst ein schönes Vaterland	*Once I had a beautiful fatherland*
Das küsste mich auf deutsch und sprach	*that kissed me in German and spoke,*
auf deutsch	*in German,*
(Man glaubt es kaum	*the words (it was almost unbelievable*
Wie gut es klang) das Wort: "Ich liebe dich!"	*that they could ring true), "I love thee!"*
Es war ein Traum.	*It was a dream.*

despised religion he had been unable to matriculate in a
university or take a degree, although his presence at the
German University of Prague—on back benches—had
been tolerated). More than once, he had known jail as a
Jew and a liberal. Worst of all, perhaps, he regularly attended the conferences of the Reform movement and had
accepted early Jewish Reform's basic command that the
Jews relinquish the isolation of their tight little medieval
world and its summons to pious resignation. Radnice's Jews
were provincial, traditional, and submissive. Overburdened
by the crushing problem of sheer survival, they wished only
to be left unnoticed as they followed their ancient customs
and clung precariously to whatever could be called home.

For all that he "never had a fatherland," Wise was
thoroughly representative of that majestic parade of scholars, scientists, and artists that the small but supremely
talented German-Jewish community contributed to modern
civilization during the brief period in which its existence
was tolerated. Paradoxically enough, his confident and optimistic world outlook underlay his judgment that in
Europe neither Judaism nor the spirit of man in general
could expand and grow. He could see—and demand—a
future when others saw only a cautious present and grim
past. His eagerness to realize the progress that he saw was
possible exceeded the abilities of people with lesser vision
to follow him. Born to lead, and with a profound sense of
mission, he often, both in youth and in later life, pressed
forward so determinedly and so fast that he lost contact
with his following, ending up a general without an army.
Reform Judaism continued to make its way in German
cities and human rights and modern life to spread across
German lands, in the wake of industrialization and the

revolutionary uprisings of 1848. By 1848, however, Wise had been in America for two years, having written off Europe completely. But who can say that he was wrong and that Jews who shared his aspirations but stayed on in Germany and Austria were right? Certainly, civil rights and high place in finance, commerce, and cultural life for German Jews were evanescent phenomena. They did not protect Jews from the most virulent and deadly antisemitism, which resulted, twenty-five years ago, in the murder factories of Auschwitz and Belsen and the obliteration of sixteen centuries of Jewish life between the Rhine and the Vistula.

While still in Europe, Wise fell in love with America. He regarded himself as, spiritually, an American. He loved America's egalitarianism; her common, public education; her noninterference with religion; her commitment to humanity's forward march. The Jews had been accepted in America for two centuries, and lived there in dignity and honor. Even now, Jewish emigrants from Germany and Poland were streaming to the United States by the thousands and building lives of the kind denied to them in the countries of their origin. In America there were no ghettos. The Jews could own homes, work on the land, and hold up their heads in honored partnership with their gentile neighbors. Here, if anywhere, was the Promised Land, the New Zion. In America the Jewish religion could renew itself, shaped by the rationalism of the age and purged of persistent tribalism, mysticism, and superstition, opening outward toward the world of science and nature, nevermore spiraling inward in isolation and despair.

America, the American Reform-Judaism-to-be, and Isaac Mayer Wise were all made for one another, it seemed. Theresa Bloch Wise, Isaac Mayer's wife, felt differently, however. To her, America was a savage land of murderous Indians, illiterate backwoodsmen, and crude log huts; she feared to rear her infant daughter in such surroundings. But her husband was determined to emigrate. He was determined, also, to be an American in America, not a transplanted Sudeten-German rabbi ministering to a small group isolated from the larger American population by a foreign language and culture. He redoubled his study of English, both spoken and written. Soon his literary English, already fluent, was to be irreproachable in grammar and syntax and quite stylish—to the end of his life it would be florid, stately, and quaintly Victorian. With his family, he landed in New York in 1846. He never saw Europe again.

In America, Wise found 60,000 fellow Jews. A few thousand, chiefly Spanish-Portuguese, were of pre-Revolutionary stock. Most were German or Polish immigrants from the post-Napoleonic wave that began in 1816 and continued till after the Civil War. They were not a coherent group, being organized only on the level of the individual congregation, which, again, was formed according to territorial origin—Bavarian, Prussian, Austrian, Polish, Hungarian, Spanish-Portuguese, and so on. Three congregations—Beth Elohim in Charleston, Har Sinai in Baltimore, Emanu-El in New York—had been chartered as Reform institutions. But the bulk of Jews in America were attached to Orthodox rituals, even though, in quick response to the economic demands of their environment, they were dropping many practices that were irksome to observe. What Jewish learning there was had been brought over by the Germans. In Revolutionary times Jewish learning was so conspicuously absent that Aaron Lopez, the Newport merchant, found it impossible to get a letter in Hebrew translated in his own community and was forced to repair to President Ezra Stiles of Yale.

From his vantage point of rabbi of the little congregation of Beth El, Albany, an appointment that he received shortly after his arrival in the New World, Wise proposed nothing less than to inspire and unite this divided and refractory mass, forging the new Judaism that he had already envisaged in Europe. He was indefatigable in applying himself to this task; however, the first generation of German immigrants was a hard nut. It took more than a quarter-century for the American experience to have a decisive effect on the Jewish way of life and Jewish institutions. Accordingly, in the '70s and '80s, success came his way with an ease and smoothness amazing to anyone acquainted with his struggles of the '50s and '60s.

A passage from his *Reminiscences* shows his own formulation of the problem before him at the time of his arrival in America, and his proposed solution:

The Bavarian had to hate, or, at least, mock and revile the Hessian; both of them the Saxon, each of these the Prussian, and all combined the Austrian. This explained to me sufficiently the mutual ill-will and the incapacity of the German-Jewish congregationists to unite and work together. They were Germans who had learned the lessons of disunion and hatred thoroughly under the tutelage of thirty-six rulers....It was very plain to me that the Jew had brought all these characteristics from the old country....

The century-long oppression has demoralized the German and Polish Jew and robbed him of his self-respect. He has no self-respect, no pride left. The hep-heps of time still weigh him down; he bows and scrapes, he crawls and cringes. The Jew respects not the fellow man in other Jews, because he lacks the consciousness of man in himself. He parodies and imitates, because he has lost himself. After diagnosing this evil, I set myself to seeking a remedy.

The Jew must be Americanized, I said to myself, for every German book, every German word reminds him of the old disgrace. If he continues under German influences as they are now in this country, he must become either a bigot or an atheist, a satellite or tyrant. He will never be aroused to self-consciousness or to independent thought. The Jew must become an American, in order to gain the proud self-consciousness of the free-born man. From that hour I began to Americanize with all my might, and was as enthusiastic for this as I was for reform. Since then, as a matter of course, the German element here, as well as in Germany, has completely changed, although Judeophobia and uncouthness have survived in many; but at that time it appeared to me that there was but one remedy that would prove effective for my co-religionists and that was to Americanize them thoroughly. We must be not only American citizens, but become Americans through and through outside the synagogue. This was my cry then and many years thereafter. This, too, increased the hatred of my opponents considerably.

"But, if I succeed in Americanizing my co-religionists, will not Judaism disappear in Americanism," I asked myself, "even as the native Jewish element has approached the different sects so closely in various localities? This must be counteracted by a better knowledge of Jewish history and Jewish sources."

Wise lost no time in instituting his reforms, which, from the outset, generated commotion. He organized a choir. "Poor as the choir was, it still was the immediate means of our getting rid of all the mediaeval rubbish at once." For, in reorganizing and Americanizing the service, Wise eliminated prayers with cabalistic elements or references to a personal Messiah. Hymns were sung in English and German—neither of them, unlike Hebrew, a "holy language." The congregation was appalled when its rabbi, after the sudden death of his two-year-old daughter Laura, refused to honor the custom of wearing torn garments and sitting on the floor. He became an even more controversial figure as the result of an article he wrote for *Occident*, a magazine of Jewish interest published by the Orthodox leader Isaac Leeser of Philadelphia. The article was a spirited reply to a clergyman who invited American Jews to enter the Presbyterian fold in a body. In it, however, Wise did more violence to the tenets of belief of his unreformed coreligionists than to those of his gentile adversary. "I had to administer orthodox Judaism almost as many blows as orthodox Christianity," he wrote of the article later. "Miracles were not wonderful nor marvelous for me, and the Messiah was dismissed as a poetical fancy." Again, in a debate with Rabbi Morris Raphall of Charleston over Reform versus Orthodoxy, he answered no to two questions put him by his opponent: Do you believe in the personal Messiah? Do you believe in the bodily resurrection? Raphall rushed out of the room. Shortly thereafter he published an article demanding Wise's dismissal from the pulpit. Remarkably enough, after all this, the crisis that finally split the Albany synagogue and produced a scandalous riot at the Jewish New Year services in 1850 resulted not from Wise's unorthodoxy but from his demand that a board member keep the Sabbath or resign.

Wise's views received wide circulation and were hailed by liberal Protestant leaders, notably the Boston Unitarians William Ellery Channing and Theodore Parker. The rationalism that was transforming Judaism was having a like effect on the spiritual thinking of the Christian community. Channing and Parker, for example, rejected such ancestral Calvinist doctrines as the original sin of all mankind and eternal damnation of the wicked, and projected a universal religion with an ethical, rationalist, and humanist core. In addition, in Protestantism as a whole there was a strong Judaizing tendency—stronger by far in America than in the Old World—and there was eagerness on the part of the general community to meet the people of the Old Testament on common ground. Under those circumstances, it was inevitable that the resemblances between Judaism and Christianity would loom large and that both religions would be seen in their common aspects. Wise himself returned to this subject again and again, among other places in his *Reminiscences*, where he gives an account of an extended conversation in Washington with Daniel Webster, then Congressman from Massachusetts and a prominent lay Unitarian; Judah P. Benjamin, a Spanish-Portuguese Jew, Senator from Louisiana, and, later, successively Attorney General, Secretary of War, and Secretary of State for the Confederacy; and Navy Lieutenant Mathew Fontaine Maury, one of America's great scientists of all time and the father of oceanography. The talks began in Webster's office and finished in Willard's Hotel.

"Mr. Senator," said Webster to Benjamin, "my friend is of your race. I would have said your co-religionist, but I do not know how much or little you believe; and in truth we are all co-religionists, since we are all Unitarians."

Maury had never belonged to any organization or confessed a faith. Benjamin said Judaism and Unitarianism were different....

Webster began the interrupted conversation at once, and wanted to know my opinions. I referred to Theodore Parker's conception of Unitarianism, and set over against this my conception of Judaism. This forced me to the conclusion that there was no essential difference in the matter of doctrine, but in historical development, which, however, did not enter into the matter of doctrine. "It is well," said Webster, extending his hand to me. "You are indeed my co-religionist." Maury made the droll confession that he believed something of the same kind, but had never had time to give it a definite form.

Wise's ideas about the historical development that both joined and separated the two religions were expressed at length, throughout his life, in numerous lectures and publications, and in brief in 1899, at a celebration honoring his eightieth birthday. "The teachings of Reform Judaism," he said on that occasion, "will be the religion of the twentieth century."

Let us take note here of the qualifying word "teachings." Wise was not expecting anything so simple-minded as the mass conversion of the huge Christian-American majority. Rather, with his belief in the dynamics of progress —this child of the Enlightenment could hardly think otherwise—he expected a continuous evolution of Judaism and Christianity both toward the redemption of mankind and ultimate fulfillment of the covenant made on Mount Sinai between God and the children of Israel. He accepted literally and without reservation the Sinaitic revelation of the Law and the mission of the Jewish people to the world as a "kingdom of priests and an holy nation." Just as Judaism was evolving into a universal religion through the elimination of rabbinism and cabalism, Christianity, he believed, in its development toward ever higher levels, was attenuating Christology. This was the key to the progress of Christian thought and therefore to the creed of future men—the purest substance of the revelation on Mount Sinai.

Wise took a major step forward in his life when he became rabbi of Bene Jeshurun, Cincinnati, in 1854. For the forty-six years until his death, his relation with that congregation was more than harmonious: it was a love affair from

the beginning. The congregation built him a huge temple
on Plum Street, paid off the mortgage on his farm property, provided him with a town house, and increased his
salary when congregations in large Eastern cities tried to
lure him away. Wise, in return, worked tirelessly—editing,
organizing, writing, lecturing. He planned great institutions, and they arose, making this city of the Old Northwest
the mecca of Reform Judaism.

Simultaneously, in 1855, he organized a publishing
house, Bloch and Company, with his brother-in-law; established two vigorous weeklies, the English-language
American Israelite and the German-language *Die Deborah*;
and, together with Rabbis Kalisch and Rothenheim, began
reform of the prayer book, drafting the *Minhag America*,
designed specifically for the modern religious conscience.
In the new ritual, the "second day" of holidays that lasted
one day in Palestine was amputated.[4] Eliminated as
anachronisms were petitions for the return to the land of
Israel, the revival of the Temple sacrifices, and the restoration of the priesthood and the House of David. English and
German translations of Hebrew prayers were provided.
The *Minhag America* was used in the Plum Street Temple
for 39 years, and became standard in the West and South.
Wise would have preferred a ritual designed by a representative rabbinical body. When the Central Conference of
American Rabbis—an organization of his own creation—

---

[4]The religious calendars of the Jewish communities scattered over the Roman
Empire were regulated from Palestine. In later times, the non-Palestinian Jews no
longer received such instructions; nevertheless, they tried to keep Land of Israel time
in their religious life. Inasmuch as the sun set and rose from one to four hours later in
European lands, European Jews assured themselves of "synchronization" by adding 24
hours to every period of observance, except for fast days, whose rigors would have become excessive.

produced such an order of service in 1894, Wise cheerfully replaced the *Minhag America* with the *Union Prayer Book*.

Also in 1855, the opportunity arose to move toward realization of a persistent dream: the organizational union of America's Jews. Much of the Jewish world today owes its very existence to the high degree of organization of American Jewish life—the continuing legacy of Isaac Mayer Wise. The 1855 conference was at Cleveland, where Orthodox delegates insisted on a pledge of adherence to the "traditional, legal, and logical exposition of the Biblical laws which must be expounded according to the Talmud." Union was as important to Wise as reform. Convinced that life itself would impose the shape of Reform on whatever institutions would be developed under American conditions, Wise was willing to accept this paragraph. However, the distinguished theologian David Einhorn of Baltimore, who was also a pioneer of Reform but more deeply concerned with doctrines and ideas than with organization, reacted angrily toward any compromise with Talmudism. The Orthodox, too, were dissatisfied, finding the conference too progressive, Talmud paragraph or no. Union, thus, became wrecked between the forces of two extremes. In spite of his disappointment, Wise maintained pressure for union in the pages of the *Israelite*. He gradually lost conviction that union was possible between Orthodox and Reform, and even between Reform and Reform if his Eastern opponents were to be included. In 1873, Reform congregations from the West and South, where his influence was preponderant, created the Union of American Hebrew Congregations. The Eastern congregations joined five years later. Soon, his leadership was unchallengeable and unchallenged, and in 1889 the Central Conference of

American Rabbis was brought into existence in Detroit.

The convention that established the Union of American Hebrew Congregations declared that its first object was to organize a "Hebrew Theological College to preserve Judaism intact, to bequeath it in its purity and sublimity to posterity, to Israel united and fraternized." In 1875, with the foundation of Hebrew Union College in Cincinnati, this hope became a reality. For many years, Wise had urged that American rabbis be American-trained—before HUC was in operation, young men had been sent to Germany for their rabbinical studies. He believed that American Judaism would be represented unworthily by men who were not thoroughly immersed in the free spirit of American institutions.

The College's beginnings were not impressive. Wise was the unpaid president and half the faculty; the students were all preseminarists and no more than children—"four of them wanted to study; ten wanted to make noise." The entire library "was locked up in a two-and-one-half-foot box, not because of thieves but because of mice." But it was a triumphant moment, in 1883, when the first ordination took place and four young rabbis received the kiss of consecration.

Today the College is a truly majestic institute of learning, with an impressive physical establishment that includes a library of 160,000 volumes, a museum, and the very extensive American Jewish Archives. The Jewish Institute of Religion, New York, merged with Hebrew Union College in 1948, and there is now a branch of the College in Los Angeles. In keeping with today's expanded needs, there is an increasing national demand for well-trained cantors and religious school teachers; and the School of Education and Sacred Music has been added to the New York campus.

Although Wise saw his Hebrew Union College and Union of American Hebrew Congregations prosper and grow, he was to get a Pisgah view only of the Promised Land in the New World. Between 1880 and Wise's death in 1900, a torrent of refugees from Russian, Polish, and Romanian pogroms swelled the Jewish population to several millions. The newcomers, still immersed in the Middle Ages, were like visitors from another planet. They huddled together in congested ghettos, practicing unfamiliar and apparently outlandish customs. To a country still fundamentally Anglo-Saxon in composition, they seemed utterly incompatible. The vastly expanded Jewish community ceased to be adapted to the American environment and entered a new period of instability.

Orthodox rabbis, of course, were included among the immigrants from Eastern Europe. Unlike their counterparts in the already established and Americanized Jewish community, they did not try to link their people with the manners, customs, and institutions of their new world. On the contrary, they set themselves against accommodation and change, exerting all the power at their command to preserve unaltered the medieval Judaism they had brought along with them. This, of course, was like commanding the tides to stand still. The pull of modern life was too strong for all but a contingent of comparative zealots. Thus, a vacuum of leadership was created in the transition of the Eastern European arrivals from Old World to New World ways. Isaac Mayer Wise, among others, saw in this situation a challenge to the Reform rabbinate to provide constructive leadership for orderly change through substituting

his own pattern of American Judaism for the receding mi-
grant religion and culture. But this consummation of his
endeavors would have to be a task for another generation.
There was aptness in the text that Judah Magnes used at
the elder Wise's funeral service in 1900. This was the last
chapter of *Deuteronomy*, the biblical account of the death
of Moses. The fourth verse reads as follows:

> And the Lord said unto him, This is the land which
> I sware unto Abraham, unto Isaac, and unto Jacob,
> saying, I will give it unto thy seed: I have caused
> thee to see it with thine eyes, but thou shalt not go
> over thither.

The stabilization of the Jewish community and the
advancement of American Judaism were responsibilities
assumed by Wise's spiritual descendants, the American-
educated Reform rabbinate of the twentieth century. Jonah
Bondi Wise, Isaac Mayer Wise's son, played a leading role
—a Joshua to his father's Moses.

✡ II ✡

Cincinnati

THE OLD WISE FARM ON NORTH COLLEGE HILL is half a mile from the Cincinnati city line—today, less than an hour's drive from the downtown business section. The relentless march of urbanization has left only the farmhouse and a small strip of land from its original 38 acres. The rest of the property has become a large suburban shopping center dominated by a big Sears Roebuck department store. In winter the plows come out as soon as a snowflake hits the ground, and the roads stay clear. No one in the area needs to move into the city for fear of being snowbound.

Things were otherwise in the '70s and '80s of the last century, when the four children of Rabbi Isaac Mayer Wise and his young second wife, Selma Bondi, were born.

In the winter of 1880-81, as in the previous few years, the Wises moved to their town house early, before snow could make the roads near College Hill difficult of passage. Selma was expecting her second child. When childbirth was imminent, she and her husband moved to two or three rooms on the second floor of the old Hexter Hotel in downtown Cincinnati in order to avoid disrupting the crowded house at 126 Dayton Street. Hexter's was a ramshackle structure, low, rambling, and nondescript in style, but much beloved in the German community, for which it was a popular social center. Isaac Mayer Wise spent many Saturday evenings at Hexter's drinking beer with his cronies.

Selma Bondi's expectations of a child were exceeded, and, on February 21, 1881, twin children were born to her —Jonah Bondi and Regina Wise.

Selma was extremely strong-willed and healthy. However, even she could not cope with the enormous platter of corned beef and cabbage that Hexter's kitchen, with an unshakable faith in the universal efficacy of hearty fare, sent to her room the evening following the birth of the twins. She sent it back, requesting soft-boiled eggs. But the following morning she was sitting up in bed industriously making diapers, of which she had only half the needed supply.

The Bondi family, as the name itself would indicate, was Sephardic in origin. Rabbi Yom Tob Bondi of Seville, presumably as a result of the expulsion of the Jews from Spain in 1492, settled in Italy, where the name Bondi is still frequent. Around 1600, the Bondis moved to Prague, and, around 1750, to Dresden, where Simon Bondi became fiscal agent to the court of Saxony and Poland. Descendants of a Mainz branch of the family lived in Germany until the advent of Hitler, and, since, have been dispersed in England, America, and Israel.

In 1859, Jonas Bondi of Dresden became the first of the family to emigrate to the New World. He practiced his calling of rabbi for a year, and at the end of that time became the publisher of a German-language periodical in New York. Jonas was Jonah Wise's grandfather and, through the marriage of his wife's father, Marcus Raabe, to Salomon Heine's widow, was step-brother-in-law to Heinrich Heine, first cousin and namesake of the great German poet. In Dresden, it had been Jonas Bondi's pleasant custom to educate his three daughters in languages by rotating the nationality of their governess—an English governess one year, a French governess the next, and so on. The girls became well versed in the English, French, and German classics though they had little or no foundation in science and mathematics. In the United States, one of them, Bianca—later Bianca Robitscher, the young Jonah Wise's favorite aunt—became the first woman graduate of Cooper Union and a portrait painter of some distinction. Jonas Bondi was also the owner of the finest private library of Judaica in the United States.

In 1876, two-years widowed and still grieving, Isaac Mayer Wise visited New York in order to inspect the famous library, which was now for sale because of its owner's recent death, and to acquire it for the newly founded Hebrew Union College. It took him only six weeks to secure the library for the College and the librarian—the beautiful and cultivated Miss Selma Bondi—for himself. He announced his second marriage April 28, 1876, in an advertisement in the *American Israelite*, his English-language periodical. This advertisement read as follows:

The editor of the *American Israelite* has entered upon a life co-partnership with Miss Selma Bondi, of New York, the daughter of the late Rev. Jonas Bondi, editor of the *Jewish Leader*. The articles of agreement were signed, sealed, and delivered, Monday, April 24th, in presence of Dr. Joseph Lewi and Lady, of Albany, N.Y., and various other ladies and gentlemen interested in the new firm. Rev. Dr. A. Huebsch, of New York, performed the ceremonies, and the Doctor's excellent lady said the necessary responses. The capital invested in the said firm to be known hereafter as Isaac M. Wise & Lady, consists of all the editorial and directing abilities of the first party, and the executive and corrective abilities of the second party. The firm to be dissolved by mutual consent three days after death. It is understood that Dr. Wise will attend to editorial and outside business as heretofore, and Mrs. Selma Wise will direct the home affairs at 126 Dayton Street. In regard to sermons, it has been agreed that Dr. Wise continues to preach the sermons and deliver the lectures in the temple, and Mrs. Selma retains the privilege of delivering occasional curtain lectures; profits or losses to be shared equally, and no papers to be accepted or indorsed, especially no love-letters, except by mutual knowledge and express consent. Friends are politely invited to call and inspect the new establishment.

The high good humor of this playful announcement made it, in later times, a favorite souvenir of Jonah B. Wise, who often expressed the wish that it be reprinted in full. Isaac Mayer Wise, clearly, gave a rabbinical flavor even to his jokes, here in the puzzling designation of three days after death as the term of the marriage contract. There is no precedent in Jewish tradition for this provision in the announcement. Among medieval Jews, it was sometimes the custom for a husband to give his wife a conditional divorce to take effect at death or just before it. The purpose of such a conditional divorce was to relieve a childless widow of the obligation, under Jewish law, either to marry her brother-in-law in order to provide the deceased with issue or to undergo Chalitza, a particularly degrading ceremony in which she was spat upon. Three days after death, however, is an absurdity, and was so intended by Isaac Mayer Wise.[1]

During the many years of Theresa Bloch Wise's illness and the two years subsequent to her death, Isaac Mayer Wise's affairs were in a state of confusion. The gentlest and most indulgent of fathers, he had difficulty in maintaining a suitably disciplined and orderly home for his eight children, some of whom had got very much out of hand. Now, with characteristic vigor, Selma cleaned up the farm, cleaned up her stepchildren, and provided her husband with a happy, smoothly running home. Soon she had four children of her own: Elsie, the twins Jonah and Regina, and Isaac, Jr.

Jonah was a handsome boy with dark, luminous eyes in a sensitive face—slight of build but an accomplished, graceful athlete. Happy and outgoing, with something of his father's charm, he made friends effortlessly. Everything came easily to him. As a toddler, he gave himself the appellation "Dode"—a childish attempt to say "Jonah"—and Dode he was to his intimates for the rest of his days. His twin Regina, by the same token, was "Rags." He used to hold her hand to give her needed assurance when they were in the long, dark, spooky corridors of the Hexter Hotel. When Jonah was eight, the congregation presented Isaac Mayer Wise with a larger house at 615 Mound Street on the occasion of his seventieth birthday.

Jonah had little time to himself as a young boy. He attended public school in the mornings and children's classes at Hebrew Union College—then on Sixth Street,

---

[1]For this interpretation I am indebted to Dr. Solomon B. Freehof of Pittsburgh, a leading authority on Jewish law.

three blocks away—in the afternoons. The Hebrew lessons were followed by piano lessons, held in the music room, next to Isaac Mayer Wise's library. Jonah was interested in music all his life, but, apparently, was an indifferent performer; his poor father, time after time, crept out of the library and gave him a dime not to practice any more. In consequence, Jonah's repertoire was confined to a single waltz. The tedium of study was lightened by a running exchange of youthful wit and banter—much as lesson preparation today takes place against a background of radio program or telecast—and listeners could hear quip after quip followed by a chorus of groans.

Close family life made up for lack of excitement. For recreation there was little to do but read. Jonah read constantly. Sometimes, to his father's horror, he and Regina were seen with *Golden Days*, a publication inoffensive to twentieth-century sensibilities but regarded by the elder Wises as the height of sensationalism. For the most part, he read big, solid books. He was particularly fond of history, and had read Green's *England* before entering high school. His father gave him the run of the five thousand volumes in the library at Mound Street, especially feeding him Dickens and Thackeray. Isaac Mayer Wise was himself a novelist, albeit of no great distinction, and these were his admired models. The old man worked tirelessly at a big table in the library, writing by hand with a steel pen on big sheets of yellow paper while the boy sat nearby or even read on the floor, sometimes falling asleep at his father's feet.

In the middle grades the Wise children attended a one-room country school, all eight grades of which were taught by a Mr. William Jones, who had come to Ohio directly from college in Massachusetts. Isaac Mayer Wise had donated the property for the schoolhouse. After it was built, he received the surprise of being voted off the board of trustees. Among Jonah's schoolmates was Charles Robinson, a Negro boy and son of the farmer who worked the Wise farm on College Hill. Cincinnati is in the southernmost part of Ohio, just over the Ohio River from the Southern state of Kentucky. That region of Ohio was a part of the old Northwest territory settled, in the decades following the American Revolution, by the Ohio Company, an antislavery corporation chartered in Massachusetts. White people and Negroes lived there on a traditional basis of equality and freedom from prejudice. Charles and Jonah were good friends and playmates in school and on the farm. They had occasion to renew their friendship in later years, when Jonah was rabbi of Central Synagogue, New York, and Charles was a Pullman porter and a preacher in Harlem. Another schoolmate was Clarence Cary, great-nephew of the mid-nineteenth-century poets Alice and Phoebe Cary.

Summers were spent on the farm, which was heaven to every member of the family, each for his own reasons. Isaac Mayer Wise was proud of being a landowner, a status he had been denied in Europe because of his Jewish religion. In later years, Jonah described his own existence on the farm as Tom Sawyer-like. He saw the farm as a whole world whose tastes and flavors had been revealed to him in his reading and re-reading of *The Adventures of Tom Sawyer, Life on the Mississippi, Huckleberry Finn*, and other books by Mark Twain. For him, the farm established a connection with the earlier, freer, simpler, and wilder life of the ante-bellum American frontier. The spirit of that life he tried to recapture in strenuous physical play in which he was always the leader and the breathless followers were Regina, young

Isaac, Charlie Robinson, and Ida and Sidney Bernheim—
Ida and Sidney were his niece and nephew, although almost
exactly his own age. There were fishing and swimming in
the creek near the pasture, and Jonah was always building
rafts, in keeping with his picture of himself as Tom Sawyer.
While he was in college, in fact, he still kept a raft on the
creek, the *Stella S.* His exertions on the farm hardened and
matured his young body. His considerable athletic accomplishments in high school, college, and later life, he always
felt, were largely owing to this central experience of his
youth.

The farm was full of people. Isaac Mayer Wise used to
bring teachers from Hebrew Union College to vacation
there. Since he had twelve children of his own, to say nothing of sons- and daughters-in-law and grandchildren, the
congestion at the farmhouse sometimes reached epic pro-
portions.

There was ample food for this multitude, for the farm
was well-stocked and efficiently run. Tall chestnut trees
lined the carriage drive that led to the crabapple trees,
flowering shrubs, and flower beds of the well-shaded front
yard. To the south were the apple orchard and raspberry
patch. Feed crops for the cows, horses, and poultry were
raised on the large fields on both sides of the creek beyond.
Behind the house was the vegetable garden, which had a
row of hotbeds to raise plants from seed. East of the garden
was a grove of peach trees, famous for the magnificence of
their fruit. Above the pasture on the hillside were the pear
orchard and the vineyard. The vineyard supplied the table
with Catawba grapes and fine claret wine. Beechnuts,
hickory nuts, and walnuts were provided by the woodlot at
the extreme southeastern part of the property.

Max B. May, Isaac Mayer Wise's grandson through his oldest daughter, Emily, has left a nostalgic note on life at the Wise farm.

Well do I remember how my mother would supervise the churning of the butter, for the butter was really noted for its excellence. An icebox was in the cellar, and the milk would be put into crocks and put into the icebox. My mother would, during the day, skim the cream, some of which she would put away for table use— the bulk of the cream was put into vessels that contained the cream to be used for butter. Churning was done twice a week. Our buttermilk was famous. When the milk soured, much of it went to feed the poultry, the rest to make cottage cheese. My mother used to allow a certain amount of the cream to ferment, and, when it had sufficiently fermented, she would boil it and, after using much butter and caraway seed, she would put the liquid cheese in molds to dry. This cheese was called "hedge cheese," sometimes "gekochte kaese." I doubt whether you could buy at this time a cheese so wonderful.

Isaac Mayer Wise was an expert in raising sweet corn, and even grew his own seed. Various plots on the farm were marked off to be planted at two-week intervals through the growing season, so that from July through September there was always a supply of young, tender corn. Through his father, Jonah, too, learned to feel close to the soil and to love growing things. Fishing, golfing, and tramping through the woods were an integral part of his life in later years and kept him on even keel throughout periods of the greatest stress. When advancing age circumscribed his athletic activities, he turned to growing things once more, becoming, in his last years at Hartsdale, an accomplished and enthusiastic gardener.

*   *   *

Jonah attended the Hughes High School in Cincinnati for four happy years, simultaneously pursuing studies at Hebrew Union College. Among his intimates in the Hughes High class of 68 persons with whom he graduated in 1899 were Otto Rosenberg, now of New York, Stella Schottenfels, and Gilbert Bettman. Bettman, a judge in Cincinnati, later married Jonah's niece Iphigene, the daughter of Helen Wise Molony. Bettman's son Gilbert is the present owner of the old Wise farm property.

At school, Jonah was too engrossed in extracurricular activities to be more than an average student. He played football and baseball, ran the 220-yard dash, took part in every performance of the dramatic society, and belonged to a fraternity known in Latin as the "Triginta Optimi"— "the thirty best." He is described by classmates as having had a sharp, witty tongue and as having been willing to do almost anything for a laugh. Above all, through the magnetism of his personality, with which he dazzled students and teachers alike, he assumed active control of all student activities. All his life he was to be a spellbinder—not so much with big audiences or on state occasions, which made him withdraw a little within himself, as with small groups and on informal occasions. He was devoted to his more intimate schoolmates, as they were to him. His prime interest was in people, and he had a natural talent for friendship and an irresistible urge to lead.

Jonah came by his wit honestly. His father was a witty man. In Cincinnati, in the '90s, travelers on Jewish errands dined Sundays at the Wise family table. Once the guest was a *mohel*, officiator over the ancient rite of circumcising males on the eighth day after birth. The *mohel* complained that modern parents wanted doctors—it was more sanitary.

"Nonsense," boomed I.M. Wise. "What can you catch from a baby that small?"

Isaac Mayer Wise's wit sometimes took a bitter turn. Of Emil Hirsch, a tenacious opponent in Jewish affairs, he once remarked, "I don't see why that man speaks ill of me; I never did him a favor."

Jonah's last year at Hughes High was saddened by the death of his strikingly beautiful older sister, Elsie, who died of meningitis after months of suffering. She had gleaming red-gold hair, and, after her death, Jonah was to have a particularly soft spot in his heart for any girl whose hair reminded him of Elsie's. He named his first daughter after her.

In 1900, Rabbi Isaac Mayer Wise died. He had a Hebrew Union College class and preached a sermon on the Saturday that he received a paralytic stroke, breathing his last on Monday evening. Had he died four or five years later, Jonah might have gravitated toward journalism or the law and never have become a rabbi. Neither at high school nor, later, in his first years in college, did he give any sign of favoring such a vocation. His father had never urged any of his sons to enter the rabbinate. Jonah's friends, in fact, had every expectation that he would eventually be a lawyer or a journalist. Here it must be said that attendance at Hebrew Union College was of no great relevance; this, among the German and Polish Jewish middle-class families of Cincinnati, in the '80s and '90s, was regarded as part of general education. Selma Wise, however, as the widow of the leading religious leader of the Mississippi Valley and the descendant of a rabbinical line three centuries old, was concerned that one of her sons carry on this double tradition. The death of Isaac Mayer Wise brought this concern to the foreground of her awareness. Jonah's talents for leadership were already in evidence. He had the easy charm of the natural aristocrat, and almost everyone found him completely captivating. Jonah, she felt, was a fitting candidate for this role. She began, first, to exercise her powers of persuasion upon him to become a rabbi, and, then, to sacrifice, scrimp, and save so that his years of American education could be crowned by final study in Europe.

"It would take the whole Annual to say all the things that might be said of Dodie," reads the University of Cincinnati yearbook for 1903. "He has always stood for patriotism and school spirit." And his listed activities were formidable indeed: class football team and varsity track team his freshman and sophomore years; athletic council president, varsity football team, 1902 carnival committee, and class president his junior year; students' executive committee, 1903 carnival committee, forum president, and editor of the university newspaper his senior year. He had little time to participate in dramatics, but could not resist playing Jaques in *As You Like It*, the senior play.

On the campus, Jonah, followed by his Irish setter Cleopatra, was perhaps the most familiar figure. He was the leader of the "Barbs," or Barbarians, the students who were not affiliated with Greek-letter societies. Among his lieutenants were Herman Baylis, Henry Bentley, and Anna Bird Stewart. There was always an active contest between Greeks and Barbs for control over campus activities and organizations. As Jonah's list of offices and honors would indicate, this contest was distinctly one-sided during his four years of residence at the university. The principal means of maintaining Barb domination was a thoroughly organized and highly efficient political team whose job was to cultivate freshmen and win them away from the opposition. Jonah cheerfully labeled them the "steal trust."

Jonah's chosen course of study at the university would probably not be tolerated at colleges today, which, in keeping with the times, are oriented toward science. Jonah's only concession toward the sciences was a half-course in biology. Otherwise, he confined himself to social studies, philosophy, and ancient and modern languages and literatures. He majored in history and economics. An influential teacher was J. Tucker Murray, later a professor at Harvard and, still later, head of the Folger Library in Washington, the great depository of Shakespeare's works and center of Shakespearean studies. In years to come, Jonah's theater companions would be astounded, at every performance of a play by Shakespeare, to hear him softly recite each part in time with the actor on the stage. He knew every line of every play.

Dr. Leon Watters, a young instructor in chemistry at the University of Cincinnati while Jonah was there, became his good friend and, in 1926, a member of his congregation.

Jonah was also a member of the class of 1903 at Hebrew Union College. His classmates there were by no means an utterly saintly crew, too pious and dutiful to take the easy road to learning. Professor Sigmund Mannheimer taught them the psalms on Saturday afternoons during the hour before they assembled for the regular Sabbath service. Every Saturday he chose a Hebrew psalm that the entire class was to commit to memory during the ensuing week. The class sat around a long table with Professor Mannheimer at the head. Behind him was a blackboard. He was so short-sighted that he could hardly see the blackboard, near him though it was; and the class fell victim to the temptation of writing the psalm on it. As they were called upon, each in turn, they read the blackboard and rattled off the psalm perfectly. Their professor was greatly pleased with their diligence. One Saturday, however, the psalm was not too legible, and Jonah had to lean over so far to read it that he attracted Professor Mannheimer's attention. The professor turned around, saw the writing on the blackboard, and exploded. On Saturdays thereafter he carefully inspected the blackboard before calling on students to recite. Jonah did not earn the gratitude of his fellows for that afternoon's work, and it was weeks before they completely forgave him.

The year 1903 was crucial in Jonah B. Wise's life. It was then that he made the final decision to enter the rabbinate. Even more important to him than his double graduation from the University of Cincinnati and Hebrew Union College was his maiden sermon at a great metropolitan synagogue. This took place at the Plum Street Temple—his father's synagogue—on May 2.

✡ III ✡

Wanderjahr

I N THE MIDDLE AGES AND THE RENAISSANCE, a skilled crafts-
man or artist who had completed his apprenticeship was
not admitted into the company of master craftsmen or
master artists until he had spent a year of travel through the
major centers of his trade. Thus, he perfected his skills and
brought his knowledge up-to-date. This journey was known
as the *wanderjahr*. Still later, it was the custom for almost
every English gentleman to put the final polish on his education by traveling with his tutor for a year through the
great cultural centers of the Continent. This was the
"Grand Tour."

Jonah embarked upon his combination of *wanderjahr*
and Grand Tour—a graduation present from his mother—
on the Holland-America liner *Ryndam* on July 8, 1903, in
the company of his friend and Hebrew Union College class-
mate Max Merritt, now a rabbi in Los Angeles. Their plan
was first to spend a couple of months brushing up on their
German and traveling in Germany and then to enroll for

the academic year at the University of Berlin and the Lehrenanstalt für Wissenschaft des Judentums, Germany's foremost Jewish seminary.

It was a wonderful year for both young men, neither of whom had really traveled before. Jonah had visited Chicago and New York, and during holiday seasons both young men had conducted services for small-town congregations that could not afford resident rabbis, but that was all. Now they were exchanging the narrow horizon of their native American Midwest for the broad vistas of the great world beyond.

After landing in Rotterdam, Jonah and Max Merritt proceeded to Berlin, where they were joined by Julian Morgenstern, who had graduated from Hebrew Union College a year previously. Morgenstern was already embarked on the course of distinguished biblical scholarship that was to bring him the professorship of Bible at his alma mater in 1907 and the presidency from 1921 until his retirement twenty-six years later.

In Berlin they planned a walking tour of the Harz mountains, a favorite resort area of Berliners. Carrying a few articles of clothing in their rucksacks, they spent a week of tramping through the terraced, fir-clad plateaus and deep valleys of this beautiful part of the world. At the end of almost every day's journey they found a tavern at which they ate and slept, and once slept in a friendly peasant's haymow. Unfortunately, the trip was largely rainy and wet, and Jonah noted in his diary that on the whole it was "a very pretty experience but not so very enjoyable."

They came out of the Harz mountains at Nordhausen, where they separated. Morgenstern went to Heidelberg, to continue his studies for the doctorate. Merritt went to Niederstetten in Baden, where he had relatives. Jonah returned to Berlin by way of Dresden. In Berlin, he began to study in earnest in preparation for later work at the University and the Lehrenanstalt.

Long, chatty letters were sent back to Cincinnati; these, apparently, were intended to be passed from hand to hand, regardless of the addressee. Below, undated, but written late in August, is a letter to Jonah's younger brother Isaac:

Dear Ike,

Your letter was quite a surprise but very welcome. I received it in Dresden on my way home to Berlin from the Harz trip. My first experience with mountaineering was quite pleasant and very entertaining. I had projected a continuation of my journey into Bohemia to visit Steingrub, but as I could not locate it, I decided to wait until I had more definite information before attempting to venture so far.

I am glad to hear that you wish to enter the "Varsity" and know you will like it. Miss Garvin is a good friend of mine and besides being ordinarily a most obliging person, will, I am sure, if you mention my name, be able to help you a great deal. In case you enter I advise you to take History as your major and English as a minor. You will have no difficulty in getting all the credits you need in those courses. You might make Economics a minor but take my advice and do not take any of it your Freshman year. If you make History your major you are sure of many 6-hour courses which will help out wonderfully. Take 18 hours a week and you will never regret it, for you have lots of time and there is no reason you should not fill it in. Rags will of course chaperon you at first and help you out. Tell her that I liked Miss Wallack very much but could unfortunately see her for only one day and an evening as they left for London and home.

Max has gone to Niederstetten to visit relatives and Morgy has also departed, so I am home alone. My time hangs heavy sometimes but I guess I shall survive.

I touched my $500 reserve for five dollars today as I hadn't a cent in my pocket. Living here is cheap enough but books, postage and incidentals come high.

I see a good deal of Mag's friend Weil. He is a good student but a rather stupid sort of man practically. I would take his word at a "quatlat" or "quitlat" form but I would not take his oath as to the cost of bacon and eggs. I have several queer acquaintances; one talks no German but converses in Hebrew. I feel as if I shall never get intimate with that man but I can understand him a good deal better as time goes on.

At my Pension (i.e., when I take dinner) I meet nice people especially a Mr. & Mrs. Guth of San Francisco. There are shoals of Americans in Berlin but of course I have no occasion to talk to them.

Now I wish you would tell Ma that I am smitten with Dresden. It is for me a finer town than Berlin. The art Gallery is superb and the other attractions are on a par. We heard the opera Wilh. Tell in the beautiful opera house, went through the palace & Grune Gewölbe where the curios and crown jewels are exhibited and went up the Elbe to Pilnitz where we saw the King. He is a nice little old fellow with side whiskers.

Our Harz trip was of course superb. We walked over mountain and valley for miles and miles each day carrying our clothes in packs on our backs. At first the packs were heavy and galling but later became quite comfortable. We saw the beautiful Bode Thal, a Canon about 12 miles long at the end of which stand two great peaks, the Rosstraffe and Hexenstantzplatz. We climbed them both and had a great view over mountain and plain. We saw the peasants at work, mostly women, plowing with milch-cows, cutting grain with scythe & hook and being generally busy and unusual. We saw some goose herders, mostly idiotic boys it seemed. We climbed the Brocken in the rain and then saw nothing but clouds rolling below us. We parted at Nordhausen, I to Berlin and they to God knows where.

I see by Emily's letter that all are well and you may give them all a Grüss from me. Give Mam. my best love of course and so too for yourself and Rags.   Yours
                                                                    Dode

Regards to Mary and ask after her "very good health"
Letter from Ma dated 8/5th

Important $\begin{cases} \text{Don't forget Enquirer \& Israelite.} \\ \text{Subscribe from Aug. 1 for a year and have} \\ \text{them send back numbers.} \end{cases}$

This letter, in conjunction with information from
Jonah's diary, raises a fascinating question. A "Zionistic"
Congress was being held in Berlin at this time. Jonah, who,
it should be noted, subscribed to Isaac Mayer Wise's anti-
Zionist principles, attended some of the meetings and met
many of the delegates, striking up a friendship with Louis
Lipsky and Samuel Waldstein. We learn that on October
16 Jonah arranged to study modern Hebrew for three hours
a week at one mark per hour with "a nice fellow" named
Ben Jehuda. We learn further that these lessons continued
at least until the end of the year.

Who was Ben Jehuda? Was he the "queer acquaintance" who spoke Hebrew and refused to speak in German?
It would appear so. And it also would appear that he was
Ben Zion Ben Jehuda, son of Eliezer Ben Jehuda. We learn
from Robert St. John, Eliezer's biographer, that Ben Zion
was in Berlin at this time. Eliezer Ben Jehuda was a most
remarkable man and the major figure in what became
known as "cultural Zionism." He was a fanatical Hebraist
who spoke Hebrew and Hebrew only to Jew and non-Jew.
He took into his unassisted two hands the giant enterprise of
preparing a huge Hebrew dictionary oriented toward
modern life, a dictionary of the kind usually prepared by a
large team of editors and lexicographers under the auspices
of an important institution of learning. This project was
completed after his death, but during his lifetime many

volumes appeared. He may be regarded as the father of the vital national language of Israel today.

The letter to Isaac, with its reference to the Dresden art gallery, the home of the Sistine Madonna as well as of many other masterworks of the highest order, contains the first sign—soon followed by many others—of what was to be a lifelong interest in art. In the 1890s and early 1900s the Taft Museum in Cincinnati had only the meager beginnings of what is today a fine collection of works of art, unique in its holdings of medieval glass objects from Persia and the Middle East. In Jonah's youth, the opportunity to develop the cultivated taste and understanding that come from contact with great paintings and sculptures did not exist in his native city. The marvelous state collections of Germany were a revelation to him. In later years, as Edward M. M. Warburg has observed, Jonah, whenever he attended a meeting or convention, took advantage of breaks in the program to go to an art exhibition or the local museum while other delegates swapped stories or read newspapers.

The following two letters to his mother add to the picture of Jonah's life in Berlin:

August 27, 1903.

Dearest mother.

Today I feel as chipper as a grasshopper in June. I have been studying Arabic all afternoon and I hardly think that is the cause. The sausage and potato salad which I had for supper at the cost of 80 pfennig could hardly have caused it, yet I feel glad. My lamp burns more cheerfully, my room looks more cozy, and my spirit is more restful and satisfied than it has been for a long time.

I went through my regular routine today. Coffee and rolls at eight, reading, bath and swim and long stroll before dinner at 2:15. The dinner was good as it always is.

My friends Mr. & Mrs. Guth of San Francisco were as pleasant and entertaining as usual while the others, the two artist girls, talked brilliantly of the new German literature with the Russian and Greek students with an occasional opinion from Miss Radke the Hostess or the German Mr. D. After dinner I came home and worked and though no letters came from home I felt at peace with the world. It is now evening and raining as usual but I feel cozy and comfortable.

My landlady is a jewel. If I merely suggest a little thing she hustles it up in a jiffy. I get two rolls for breakfast. This morning she brought but one and said that there were no more in the house. About 15 minutes later she appeared with a second roll which she had hustled down the 5 flights of stairs to procure.

The Pollocks are still here and I see them occasionally. They are very pleasant and kind. Ed May and Setke come tomorrow or the day after.

My German letter still stands uncorrected in the letter but reproved in spirit.

I have been seeing a good deal of the Art collections and ancient relics here and expect to become quite a connoisseur. My English reading is at an end as I have read through my small stock of books exclusive of two Baedekers.

Occasionally I reread my letters and enjoy them as much as when they were new. Give my love to all who ask after me and rest assured that I am as safe and almost as comfortable as at home. Occasionally I get the "growls" but I guess I can pull through a few attacks and will finish all the better for my experience.

I would have sent these letters under separate covers but for 40 pfennig I usually get supper—sometimes for less. I am waiting for letters from the Bernheims and Leo et al before I write them again. It is hardly right that I should keep up a one-sided correspondence.

Nothing is happening here now. Max is still in Niederstetten and anything operatic or theatric is beyond my weasel-skin just now.

I want to send a special message to Stella with a promise to write her a letter. Elsa Weihl also comes in for a thought more frequently than she deserves, as she knows quite well. I must write to Sol Lowenstein and if Rags goes to the Settlement she must not forget to give my best regards to Miss Block for one hour of whose delightful conversation I would now as always give a great deal. If you or Rags see Harry Dechent give him my best and a good wish for the paper.

Tell Ike to try hard to enter the Varsity. I think it will help him a great deal.

In my camera are two plates (one good, one bad). Tell Rags to take them to the Fair and have them developed and send me a print. I also want papa's photograph.

This is a long list but I hope it won't be too onerous.

With best love
Your Loving
Son

*   *   *

Berlin, Sept. 13, 1903.
Sunday Morn.

Dearest Mamma:

Since my last home letter there has been little if anything happening that can be of any interest to you except that Max has returned. Yes, the fatted calf blew in on Friday night and in view of the importance of the occasion we got very prodigal and went out for supper. Max had been living on a strictly Kosher diet for three weeks and was simply craving a wienerschnitzel. Last night we both went to the Schiller Theater where for one mark we saw *Der Talisman* by Ludwig Fulda. We enjoyed it very much and understood it with ease. Max succeeded in getting a fairly good start in German during his stay with his relatives and insists upon "quatsching" German to me all day long.

Today is Sunday and it is quite cool but very bright and sunny. So this afternoon we shall take a long walk through the Tiergarten and call on Norrell. He came over with us and has been living in B. right along. I didn't mention it before especially as I did not see much of him. He is a very nice fellow but is about as strongminded as a weather vane. Every time I see him he asks me to umpire some quarrel he is having with himself. I usually defer decision until later and the case rarely comes up for adjudication.

We have at last solved the cold-supper problem by purchasing a spirit stove. The stove cost 7.25 M and the spirits cost 25 pfennig a liter. A liter is more than a quart. We also bought two granite cups, spoons, coffee pot & a little pot. All the outfit together cost us about 5 marks. We have cocoa and Liebig's Beef Extract on hand and last night had a big supper of Bouillon, wiener wurst, eggs and fine rolls and cocoa. We have a can of condensed milk. I have been acting as cook and have met with nothing but thunderous applause from my clientele.

Gotthold Weihl called last night while we were at supper and gassed to me for a while. He is a nice fellow and a fine student.

In a month the University opens and we are preparing our program with great care. You see we shall only be here one year and want to do the best we can.

I received a postal card from the Eckhouses who sailed last week and Mrs. E. begs me to send you her best regards. Aarron and Berkowitz were both in Berlin but I didn't see them at all. I have written New Year's cards for the first time in my life and expect that they will all come late.

At present I am O.K. and hope that you are the same. With best love to you and the children & regards to all my friends I remain

Your Loving
Son

At the time this last letter was written, Jonah and Max Merritt were living on the fifth floor of a lodging house on Brückenstrasse. Judah L. Magnes had lived there once, and Morgenstern had recommended the place on their arrival in Berlin.

The University and the Lehrenanstalt opened in October. At the University, Jonah and Max Merritt registered in the Semitics department. In addition, they enrolled in

several seminars: in history with Meyer, in philosophy with
Simmel, and in the Gospels with the famous Protestant theologian and controversial figure Adolf von Harnack, who
insisted on analyzing traditional beliefs in the light of
modern conditions and concepts and demanded the com-
pletest freedom to go wherever his thought carried him. At
the Lehrenanstalt they signed up for study with Baneth,
Elbogen, and Steinschneider.

Steinschneider taught medieval Hebrew. Jonah and
Merritt were members of a seminar that met with him once
a week—at his home, out of consideration for his advanced
age—to study Talmud. Once a week, they felt, was too
little, and on leaving Berlin their opportunities to pursue
advanced studies in Talmud were more than likely to prove
slim. Accordingly, they engaged a Russian Talmudist
named Glovinsky to read Talmud with them five days a
week.

Glovinsky was an extraordinary personality. At that
time he was 22 years old, and all his life had lived in the
Pale of Settlement, to which Russian Jews were confined
by the Tsarist government. A master in Talmud and associated studies, he had never opened a secular book. He was
mad for the secular knowledge of the world beyond the
ghetto, and had stolen his way across the Russian and
Polish borders and landed in Berlin. With an extraordinary
facility for languages and a thorough command of Yiddish,
he had learned to speak the purest German in only a few
weeks.

Many Polish and Russian immigrants in Berlin had
come there illegally, without passports, and were always in
danger of being picked up by the police. At times the police
were indifferent to such border crossings; at other times

they were under instructions to pick up all illegals. Jonah and Max Merritt studied for some weeks with Glovinsky, and then a police dragnet was put out. Much alarmed, Glovinsky came to his two students for help. He spent his days in the vicinity of the University, where the police were sparse and unwelcome, and at night sought refuge in *nachasayl*. *Nachasayl* were unregistered lodging houses where illegals could stay temporarily. Glovinsky moved from *nachasayl* to *nachasayl* to escape the attentions of the police. If arrested, he would have served a term in a German prison, after which he would have been handed over to the tender mercies of the Tsarist authorities.

Jonah proposed that he, Merritt, and William Norrell, a Protestant theological student with whom he and Merritt were on terms of the closest friendship, join together to help Glovinsky. In surrendering their passports at the university, all foreign students were given university cards. These cards made them citizens of the university while registered, and thus immune from police attention. Each of the three Americans arranged to let Glovinsky have his student card for one week out of every three. This protected Glovinsky from the police. It was a risky thing to do, but gave him several months of security. Finally, stepped-up police activity made continuance of the plan inadvisable. Reluctantly, Jonah told Glovinsky that the American students could no longer protect him with their student cards. They raised a purse and saw him off to Vienna, where life was easier than in Prussia and the police considerably more lax. They never heard from Glovinsky again, losing an interesting friend and a Talmud teacher beyond compare.

By December, Jonah and Merritt had grown cool to the

delights of wienerwurst, eggs, and cocoa prepared on a spirit stove, and decided to "go pension"—that is, to room and board with a German family. They answered a newspaper advertisement placed by a Jewish family in Potsdam, Meyer by name, consisting of husband, wife, and Erich, a five-year-old. They moved in and were pleased with the arrangement.

Herr Meyer often came to their room after dinner, before they had settled down to their evening stint of study. He loved to discuss current events with them. They welcomed his visit for the opportunity it provided to polish their conversational German. On one evening's visit, a tidal wave had just swept over a Norwegian town, which was in ruins. Emperor Wilhelm had ordered a shipload of food and medicine to be sent to the stricken town, and the Berlin newspapers were chorusing their praises of his humanity and generosity. Meyer outdid even the newspapers in the extravagance of his praise for the German monarch. Jonah listened with some impatience and remarked:

"Herr Meyer, you know this isn't pure generosity. It's a political act to gain Norwegian good will for Germany. The Emperor is a *narr*—a fool—if he thinks that he can put this over on Americans."

Herr Meyer was open-mouthed, and, a little later, left the room.

"Jonah," said Merritt, "you and I have heard often enough of *majestätsbeleidigung*, and there are quite severe penalties for it."

Jonah chose to pooh-pooh the matter, and for the time being the two young men heard nothing further.

Around Christmas, Frau Meyer took Erich for a visit to her family in Saxony, leaving Herr Meyer behind. However, the maid, a peasant girl from a nearby town, maintained Jonah and Merritt's room, and their routine lacked nothing during Frau Meyer's absence. One evening the two students were disturbed by a racket across the hall. They stepped outside their room to find Meyer pounding on the maid's door and demanding that she open it. She refused to do so.

"What's the trouble?" they asked.

Meyer, embarrassed, said that he had missed some silver and wanted to question the maid. If she would not open the door, he said, he would wait until the morning for his questioning.

All participants in the scene retired, but, in the morning, the maid told Jonah and Merritt that Meyer had tried to force his attentions upon her, and, in their presence, gave Meyer notice and asked for a favorable reference in her servant's book. Without such a reference, no German domestic could find another place. Meyer refused, and the maid packed up and left.

A week later, Jonah received a letter from Adolph Ochs, his brother-in-law and publisher of the *New York Times.* Ochs was in Vienna with Jonah's convent-educated half-sister Effie, the second-eldest surviving daughter of Isaac Mayer Wise. The Ochses wrote urging him to join them in Vienna and go on with them to Italy. A generous check was enclosed, and Jonah went. He and Merritt had made up their minds to return to Berlin, and Jonah left it to Merritt to give Herr Meyer notice and engage the new quarters before the beginning of the second semester. Merritt rented a place on Artilleriestrasse near the university, and parted company with the Meyers.

Jonah's return from his Italian vacation with the Ochses

coincided with the arrival of a note from Herr Meyer. The maid had begun an action to compel him to sign her servant's card, and Meyer had refused. His letter notified Jonah that he expected him to appear in court and that it would be to his interest to testify against the maid.

"Jonah," said Merritt, "he is threatening you with *majestätsbeleidigung*."

"Bah!" replied Jonah. "An empty threat of a medieval character."

But he consented to making sure of his ground. The following morning Merritt consulted a German lawyer with whom he had become friendly, and Jonah consulted the American consul in Berlin.

"On the mere charge of *majestätsbeleidigung* your friend can be arrested and brought into court," the lawyer said to Merritt. "Only the testimony of the man hearing the offense is needed for a court sentence to be passed. That means jail and deportation." The American consul told Jonah the same thing. On learning that Adolph Ochs was Jonah's brother-in-law, the consul immediately offered him any sum that he might require, and begged him to leave Berlin and Germany before there was any trouble. Switzerland had excellent universities, he said, and urged Jonah to consider continuing his studies in one of them. He also suggested that Jonah leave at once.

Jonah left for Berne the following evening, and Merritt sent his baggage after him. In Berne, Jonah finished the second term in what proved to be delightful surroundings.

Herr Meyer turned white when he saw Merritt, who had been summoned as a witness by the maid's lawyer, sitting alone in court. Merritt explained that Jonah was now studying in Switzerland, and his further testimony

resulted in a finding against Meyer, who was fined, required to sign the maid's servant's book, and given an
official reprimand from the bench. Jonah was more than
delighted to receive this news.

While living in Potsdam, Jonah wrote a long essay,
which he sent to his half-brother Leo's *American Israelite* in
Cincinnati. It was printed December 24, 1903, under the
title of "Anti-Semitism in Prussia," and is especially interesting as Jonah's first piece of mature journalism. In con-
trast to the careless outpouring of his epistolary style, it is
crisply written and efficiently organized. Apparently, in
spite of the fun and excitement of foreign travel and study,
he was capable of taking a hard look at his surroundings.
He wrote, in part:

The scope of this sentiment is not confined to a few classes
of individuals, but is universal throughout the whole network of
Prussian society. Officials, officers, statesmen hate the Jews.
Professors at universities lecture anti-Semitic theory from the
rostrum; the students are the strongest of this class; and so on,
down to the boy who sweeps slush from the street. Where does
it tend to lead is a matter of the utmost importance; its effect is
noticeable in two ways, both extreme—the one in Zionism,
the other in proselytizing.

Jonah himself, in later years, was to testify to the importance of his *wanderjahr* in shaping the ideas and values
that illuminated his concern for the Jewish people. All the
events of this period of his life took place against the dramatic background of the Kishinev massacre of the Jews in
Russia—government-inspired—and the Dreyfus affair in
France—also government-inspired. For the first time,
through direct contact with such representatives as the

American Louis Lipsky and Samuel Waldstein and the Europeans Glovinsky and Ben Jehuda, the young follower of Isaac Mayer Wise's "American Judaism" became profoundly aware of another world of Jewish thought and feeling. This was the Eastern European world—native or transplanted—of the Yiddish language, of Orthodox religion, of political Zionism. This was also the world of the great mass of the Jewish people.

Jonah was destined to serve some thousands of Reform Jews as a minister in progressive Jewish congregations. His services to the main body of Jews, encompassing millions of souls here and abroad, constitute his major claim to the grateful memory of the Jewish people. The sympathy and understanding that made his contribution to the welfare of the immigrant Russian-Jewish community of Portland so effective and enabled him to perform yeoman service in the salvage of European Jewry during the Hitler terror and World War II were a direct outgrowth of this key experience of his early manhood.

Chattanooga and Portland

IN CHATTANOOGA, where he succeeded Leo Mannheim as rabbi, Jonah dedicated Temple Mizpah on December 11, 1904. Chattanooga was a sleepy Southern town, quite unlike the muscular industrial city of today. In another decade, the winds of change sweeping over the country and transforming the face of American society were to have a profound effect upon this Tennessee community. Meanwhile, however, Chattanooga was a hangover from the agrarian and mercantile world of the nineteenth century. Its population consisted almost entirely of native American stock, both white and black. Its Jews, merchants and small businessmen for the most part, were few in number and conservative in temper. Jonah's half-brother Harry Wise, the youngest son of Isaac Mayer and Theresa Bloch Wise, was among them. He had come to Chattanooga in 1887, married a Texas girl, and become completely Southern. Others included Julius and Bertha—"Grandma"—Ochs. Adolph Ochs, Julius and Bertha's dynamic son, still retained ownership of the *Chattanooga Times* but no longer lived in the town. In 1896, eight years before, after buying a controlling share in the ailing *New York Times*, he had left in order to look after his new interests. Meanwhile, he had restored the *New York Times* to health, and elevated it to a position of uncontested leadership among America's newspapers.

Jonah Wise and Chattanooga were from the first ill-matched. Jonah had already shown in college an unmistakable aptitude for public affairs and a major talent for getting things done. He was filled with the desire to help people—to get a man a job, to improve conditions in his city, to educate, to further the cause of Reform Judaism. To him, a rabbi was a community leader. But there was little scope for him in Chattanooga. The congregation wanted a rabbi only for the narrow purposes of conducting services, officiating at weddings and funerals, visiting the sick, and keeping the younger generation in touch somehow with Jewish tradition. It had no desire to be stirred into social action, or, indeed, action of any kind. It had no great concern even for respectable standards of housekeeping in the synagogue. The temple, which had been built largely through Adolph Ochs's benefactions, was new and handsome, but often dusty and seldom really clean. The porter had a distaste for brooms and mops; sometimes, exasperated, Jonah swept the temple out himself. The young rabbi's liturgical inclinations were for a cleanly designed, decorous, crisply run service, with a strong, modern musical program. The congregation was accustomed to being more relaxed, and preferred to keep things that way.

The Jews of Chattanooga liked and admired their rabbi and were impressed by his energy, but, before too many months had passed, Jonah was bored and frustrated. He felt smothered even in his social life, which, like all Chattanooga's, revolved around Grandma Ochs's boundless hospitality. Sunday at Grandma Ochs's was a command performance; along with a multitude of other friends and relatives, he sat for hours at the dining table, making scant headway against an inexhaustible company dinner. Certain personal responsibilities, in the absence of a larger social role, seemed stifling. In spite of his genuine feeling for people, he had an inner core of reserve and shied away from involvement in their family problems and personal woes. He came to feel that both he and Chattanooga would be better off if Mizpah Congregation had a different spiritual leader.

To allow a year for possible growth of the harmony necessary between a rabbi and his congregation was no more than decent. At the end of the year, if still dissatisfied, he would start looking for another post in earnest. Meanwhile, he began a series of unsuccessful attempts to give up smoking, and wrote more articles for the *Israelite*.

In 1906—the year of grace being over—he let it be known that he would be receptive to offers of other positions. In February, David Marx of Atlanta wrote to him about the possibility of an appointment in Montgomery, Alabama; Jonah preached in Atlanta two weeks after receiving the letter, but did not get the appointment. On May 24 he wrote in his diary: "Apply to A. Abrahams for Brooklyn." May 28: " Letter from Abrahams acknowledging application. Not at all encouraging." June 4: "Go to New York." June 14: "Albany. Things look blue." June 15: "Preach in Albany—fair sermon, good crowd." June 17: "Am not elected." June 18: "Go to Cleveland." He did not get the Cleveland job, either.

During this odyssey, we are told, Jonah was one day joined by another railroad passenger in an observation car. "I'm out of a job" said the other man, a hardware salesman, "and having a terrible time. I've gone from one place to another looking for employment but, everywhere I look, some Jew has got there ahead of me and beaten me out." "My problem exactly," was Jonah's gloomy reply.

He was in Indianapolis over Independence Day to attend the annual sessions of the Central Conference of American Rabbis. The Reform rabbinate was then occupied with the important issue of accommodation of the expanding Conservative movement, which was developing rapidly in response to the arrival of millions of immigrant Jews during the '80s, '90s, and 1900s. The Conservatives sought to adapt Judaism to the changed conditions of American life—changed indelibly by a tremendous influx of Eastern European immigrants of medieval culture and Orthodox religious background—by renewed emphasis on talmudic teachings and traditional customs. Conservative Judaism might be described as Orthodox in form and Reform in substance. National Jewish leaders who were themselves active members of Reform congregations provided planning and major financial support for Conservative institutions. These men were in no way compromising their religious convictions. They could see that Reform Judaism could not be the immediate avenue of Americanization for the new element, for, to the still medieval Orthodox, Reform Judaism was little more than heresy. The way to Americanization, it appeared, was through an American-oriented Judaism—yes—but with strong traditional coloring. The change of designation of Reform Judaism from "American" to "Classical"—the term now applied by

Kaufmann Kohler, Isaac Mayer Wise's successor as president of Hebrew Union College—bore witness to the new
quality of American Jewish life. Clearly, Judaism in twentieth-century America was not going to be the universal
religion envisaged in the mid-nineteenth century before the
Russian-Romanian inundation. It would have a sectarian
cast and a broad spectrum of worship and belief. There
were some prominent enemies of Reform who seized the
opportunity to advocate its expulsion from the body of
Judaism. There were no genuinely irreconcilable differences between Conservatism and Reform, however.
And, accordingly, there were unity movements—after
Isaac Mayer Wise's death in 1900 there had been sugges-
tions that the Reform Hebrew Union College in Cincinnati
and the Conservative Jewish Theological Seminary in New
York be jointly administered by the same president. Much
consideration was given to calling a synod—a church council composed of Reform and Conservative members alike—
which would devote itself to the formulation of basic rules
and doctrines whose observance would be incumbent upon
all Jews of whatever religious coloring.

Jonah spoke for unity on both days of the convention.
On the first day, at the meeting of the HUC alumni association, he defended Kaufmann Kohler's policies, which
were being attacked as reactionary by a large and influential group of graduates of the college. On the second day he
gave an extended talk in favor of calling a synod. All Jews,
he felt, were Jews. At Berlin he had learned at first hand
the keenness of the Eastern Jewish hunger for a full modern
life. In spite of the intransigence of the Eastern Orthodox
rabbis who had migrated to the New World—these gentlemen opposed all accommodation to the new environment,

even the learning of English—the immigrants were ready
and eager for American life and education. They needed
little more than a helping hand, he felt, to be absorbed
rapidly into the American scene and realize their incal-
culable potential for enriching American civilization.
Religious harmony would be a step toward this most
desirable end.

His first commerce with Stephen S. Wise (to whom he
was in no way related) was to take place very soon. Their
paths would cross often in the next 43 years.

In 1906, Stephen Wise was 32 years old, but already a
national figure. He would always be better known to the
public than Jonah, who was under sentence to be confused
with his colorful namesake every day of his life. He was well
able to live with this minor indignity, which he joked about
rather often. The jokes, however, were a trifle wry.

Stephen Wise was the moving spirit of the newer trend
in Reform Judaism. He was an early and fervid political
Zionist, a charter member of the group that set up the
Zionist Organization of America in 1897, less than a year
after Theodor Herzl published *The Jewish State*. A fighter by
nature, he tried to serve Jewish needs and aspirations
through organized mass pressure, legislative action, and
the courts; with Judge Julian Mack, he set up the American
Jewish Congress in 1918. He was an outspoken critic of
Hebrew Union College under Kaufmann Kohler's administration, deploring Kohler's educational conservatism
and intolerance of Zionism; with Mack, he set up the Jewish
Institute of Religion in 1923.

Jonah adhered loyally to his father's views and was
protective toward the institutions his father had founded.
He rejected Zionism; he felt that in America Jews had no

business adopting a discrete political identity; he was committed to voluntarism in the realization of social ends and recoiled from tactics of political force; he was personally devoted to HUC, in whose alumni affairs he was extremely active, and felt that, Kohler or no, the College fulfilled its purposes as an American institution and a vessel of Judaism. But he recognized that "to every thing there is a season, and a time to every purpose." The time of changed purposes had come, and Reform Judaism could not deny them accommodation without damage to itself. So far as he could as one man, Jonah tried to forestall divisive struggle and to mediate between the new forces and the old. He threw his weight toward the making of common cause on the foundation of shared objectives. On the one hand, he used his highly developed powers of persuasion to soften the thrust of the Stephen Wise group toward revision and change. On the other, he tried to open the citadels of Reform toward acceptance of change. Thus, despite genuine differences in principles and methods, Jonah Wise and Stephen Wise were able to deal with each other on a basis of mutual liking and respect—one measure of Reform Judaism's capacity for acceptance of radical differences of opinion within its own ranks.

On September 29, 1906, Jonah entrained for Portland, Oregon, where Stephen Wise was yielding the pulpit of Temple Beth Israel in order to found the Free Synagogue in New York. The Free Synagogue was so called because Stephen Wise was resolved that even its name would make no bones about his sovereign right to speak his mind and espouse any cause.

Jonah preached trial sermons on Friday evening October 5 and Saturday morning October 6. His Friday-evening sermon, "The Mantle of Elijah," was a graceful tribute to his predecessor, whose resignation had been accepted the previous day. Saturday morning he spoke on "Turn the Other Cheek." He had Sunday supper at the home of Adolphe Wolfe, president of the temple, and was on show for the rest of the evening to members of the board of trustees and other prominent figures in Beth Israel affairs. On Monday he returned home.

This time, at last, his virtues had asserted themselves, and, on October 15, Adolphe Wolfe wired Leo Wise at the *American Israelite* in Cincinnati: "Congregation unanimously elected Rabbi Jonah Wise. Please inform him promptly."

Two weeks later, Jonah tendered his resignation in Chattanooga, to take effect November 1. His resignation was accepted with regret, and a farewell sermon and reception followed. The day after the farewell sermon he wrote in his diary: "Receive seal ring. Leave Chattanooga without a sigh. . . . Goodbye, forever."

It was not exactly forever. He returned 45 years later to officiate at the dedication of the Temple Center of the Mizpah Congregation in honor of his half-brother Harry.

Meanwhile, on November 23, in Portland, Stephen Wise installed him as Temple Beth Israel's tenth rabbi. Jonah was to remain at this post for nineteen years.

On New Year's Eve, December 31, 1906, he summed up the previous twelve months as follows:

Résumé.
I began the year rather disgruntled and in a hopeless city. Failures in Montgomery and Albany and Cleveland made me rather sore and afraid. My trip East, my experience at the Conference, my editorial scribbles, however, gave me courage, and I end the year here in Portland. My prospects are good but the

test is crucial and severe. I must marry or go to the bow wows.
I am, however, not settled in any way. Still, I am way up for a
man of 25.

On New Year's Day he wrote:

> Resolutions.
> Succeed or bust.

As Jonah rose to deliver his inaugural sermon at Temple Beth Israel, he looked even younger than his twenty-
five years. The turnout was large. Most of the audience had
not heard him when he had spoken the month before. Now
they had come to see what manner of man the trustees had
chosen to succeed Stephen S. Wise, and they strained with
anxiety for him. This boy rabbi, of course, could only be
thoroughly overshadowed by his spectacular predecessor;
but would he at least acquit himself without discredit?
Jonah's restless energies had been saving up for two years
for just such a moment. The sermon was a triumph. Soon—
in less time than would appear humanly possible, although
with the expenditure of considerable energy—he was to become the acknowledged leader of the entire Jewish community of the Pacific Northwest.

The times called for young men in the pulpit, young
men born in America and alive to contemporary needs.
With the opening of the twentieth century a new world had
come into being almost overnight. The old individualistic,
agrarian America of the previous century was gone. In its
place was an increasingly urban industrial society explod-
ing with problems: noisome slums, labor unrest, growing
monopolies, imperialist expansion, unchecked immigration, racial tensions, political corruption. The sharpest di-
visions were splitting the country deep and wide: rich and

poor, town and country, immigrant and native, the new generation and the old.

Science and technology had brought these changes, and, with their impact on the minds of men, a revolution in thought. Older generations still retained the simple faith of their ancestors, but, by the young, religion was frequently seen as little more than superstition. All the institutions of society were being re-examined and their validity and usefulness brought into question. The church and the synagogue were not exceptions. From the viewpoint of the masses of workers laboring for low wages, they were fortresses of the rich, sanctifying capital and vilifying trade unions, strikes, and other means by which laboring men sought to overcome poverty and gain a greater share of the good things in life. From the clergy and religious institutions the people demanded, not Sabbath-day sermons on points of theology, but—a full seven days a week—help with their problems, guidance in their affairs, and a voice for equity and morality in public and private life. Social protest was the order of the day.

Demands for change and practical efforts for change in the conditions of American life came not only from the newly risen radical left but from essentially conservative leaders whose social conscience had been touched—journalists like Walter Lippmann, Herbert Croly, and William Allen White; legal scholars like Louis D. Brandeis; novelists like William Howells, Stephen Crane, and Frank Norris; churchmen like Rauschenbush, Gladden, and Stephen S. Wise; social workers like Jane Addams and Lillian Wald; politicians like William Jennings Bryan, Robert La Follette, Gifford Pinchot, Theodore Roosevelt, Woodrow Wilson, and Charles Evans Hughes. The impact of the social-reform movement—"progressivism," as it was called—was tremendous. All through America, new social legislation was passed, new social institutions were established, and old, corrupt political machines were dislodged by new reform administrations.

Jonah established roots in the larger community of Portland immediately upon arrival. Two Unitarian ministers, the Reverend William G. Eliot and the Reverend Thomas L. Eliot, assisted at his installation. An agreement for joint Thanksgiving services was already in effect among Congregation Beth Israel, Congregation Ahavai Shalom, the First Universalist Society, and the First Unitarian Church. Six days later, Jonah gave the Thanksgiving sermon at the Unitarian church with great éclat. The Eliots became friends. Five years later, when they founded Reed College—the liberal arts college which has become one of the most famous educational institutions of the West Coast —Jonah became advisor to the Jewish students at Reed. Later he enlarged this operation until it included eight or ten colleges and universities as far south as Los Angeles.

John Reed—journalist, poet, communist saint, author of *Ten Days That Shook the World*, and member of the Reed family after whom Reed College was named—was in 1906–1907 a youth of nineteen and a freshman at Harvard. Reed and Jonah met for the first time during the summer of 1907. Both, through the Eliots, belonged to the coterie of Charles Erskine Scott Wood, the most brilliant lawyer in Oregon and author of *Heavenly Discourse*. Other members included Sara Bard Field, who became Wood's wife, Art and Ella Young, and William Z. Foster, who was a Socialist at the time. Later, Foster was leader of the great steel strike of 1919 and a founder of the American Communist Party.

None of these persons were revolutionists as yet, although all were involved in or sympathetic to the struggle of the workingman for union representation and improvement of miserable working and living conditions. Essentially, they were liberals and social reformers. To Jonah, their concern for the underdog was a godly attribute and a necessary counterbalance to the prevailing stubborn conservatism of the Portland environment. In his travels through the interior, he saw with his own eyes how hard the Scandinavian lumbermen worked in the logging camps of the region, for how little pay and under what primitive conditions. Their working lives were brief, and no provision was made for the time when they could no longer work.

Members of the Wood coterie functioned as a group in raising money for the defense of labor leaders, for whom Wood acted as attorney. Jonah assisted in raising money. He was an energetic and many-sided man. Like the causes for which he worked, his requests for money were many. They were almost invariably successful, however. He went straight to the places where money was and struck the exact chord—conscience or compassion. On such occasions his personality was irresistible. Many a labor leader would have been astonished had he known the actual source of the funds that bailed him out or paid his fine. Jonah was a passionate believer in the right of every man to speak his mind, and took this particular activity very seriously.

In such company, a man of God could not very well escape a little teasing. This he did not really object to, and, when it came to banter, he was fully capable of giving as good as he got. His principal gadfly was a philosophical anarchist named Dautoff, who constantly exhorted him to "stop toadying to moneybags" and to "make an honest living." Dautoff had a great sensitivity to human weakness and an instinct for the jugular. If Jonah had a weakness as a congregational pastor, it was his depth of personal reserve. He was warm, sympathetic, and outgoing, with a tremendous capacity for personal friendship with people of all kinds—department-store owners, Hebrew School students who had caught his attention, fire-eating radicals. But he avoided any show of sentiment himself and hated public emotional display—feeling, when so involved, that his privacy had been invaded. Emotional outbursts at funerals could leave him white and shaking; and after such occasions, Dautoff would say to him, "You'll never make a priest."

Every age has its challenges; and the measure of a leader is his sensitivity to the challenges of his age and the effectiveness of his response. It is interesting to observe the father-son connection as Jonah sought to ride the crest of the tidal wave of change at the same time that he sought to preserve and extend the established values of progressive Judaism, thus playing an individual role in the major task of shaping Isaac Mayer Wise's nineteenth-century religious structure to the needs of the new century. In the process, he greatly enlarged and expanded Isaac Mayer Wise's American perspectives in the four important areas of Americanization, civic service and social welfare, interfaith activity, and public relations.

The intense moral crisis of the day, as threatening to progressive Judaism as to the Protestant churches, could not be ignored. Avoiding doctrinal matters—for the new generation could not be reached by this path—Jonah lectured and counseled, rather than preached, on topics that were close to his listeners in conducting their affairs in

accord with an enlightened conscience. He let himself be
seen at socialist meetings. He met every leader of every
movement. He spoke on social justice, on business morality,
on the relationship between science and religion. He threw
himself into education, social work, and fund raising, both
for the Jewish community and for the larger community of
the Pacific Northwest. As pastor of his flock, he established
closer bonds between the temple and its congregation, in-
troducing new forms of worship, strengthening the liturgical
arts, and intensifying work with youth and with women. In
this work he called upon the teachings of the prophets and
the lessons of the ancient Hebrew writings. He emphasized
their ethical content (as did the prophets themselves) and
their applicability to daily life and current problems. To
the extent that a social reformer could, he avoided personal
involvement in party politics, feeling that this was not the
province of a minister of religion. He particularly opposed
the adoption of a political identity by the Jews, feeling that
it prevented the thorough integration of the Jewish people
in accordance with his father's vision of American Judaism.
But his major work, perhaps, was done with and for the
thousands of Jewish immigrants newly arrived in Portland
from Russia and Romania.

A vast gulf, as elsewhere, existed between Portland's
immigrant Jews, who lived a ghetto existence on the West
Side in circumstances ranging from modest to miserable,
and the more affluent members of Beth Israel and Ahavai
Sholom, who, although ultimately of German origin, were
by now of long standing in the United States and the Northwest. The fathers and grandfathers of the Jews in comfortable circumstances had spoken broken English and had
come to Portland with peddler packs upon their shoulders,

but they themselves—except for attending services on New
Year's Day and the Day of Atonement and sending their
children to Jewish rather than Christian religious school—
were indistinguishable from their gentile neighbors; and,
indeed, there was a gradual attrition of their number
through small but steady absorption by the gentile community outside. Socially, they did not accept the immigrants, and were afraid that they themselves, as Jews,
might suffer through being identified with them. Nevertheless, they shouldered without hesitation the enormous
burdens of necessary social action for the West Siders, who
outnumbered them four to one. In so doing, they were following a 250-year-old American tradition, for the Jews in
America have taken care of their own ever since they con-
tracted with the Dutch authorities of New Amsterdam in
1654 to keep any Jews from ever becoming a public charge.

Jonah became an immediate favorite of the Orthodox
Eastern European Jews. They forgave him his beardless
face, his English speech, and his heretical practices because
he did so much for them and because he never patronized
them or condescended to them. He got them jobs, worked
toward setting up adequate facilities for the Hebrew education of their children, organized Americanization classes,
and spent many hours each week in Portland's two Jewish
settlement houses, one run by the Council of Jewish
Women, the other by B'nai Brith. Together with Ben Selling, a wealthy merchant and Portland's outstanding philanthropist, he enabled many immigrants to send to Russia
and Poland for members of their families whom they had
been unable to bring with them to America.

On the second day of Jewish religious holidays—Reform Jews observe one day only—Jonah would attend

services at one of the Orthodox synagogues. These visits
were not returned too often by the Orthodox—not, at least,
by the first generation. On one of those comparatively rare
occasions, an old gentleman came to thank him for his aid
in bringing his family from Europe to Portland. Jonah paid
his guest the honor of inviting him to the altar during the
Reading of the Law. The invitation was accepted, but the
old gentleman kept his hat on, in contravention of Reform
custom. The beadle, white-faced, ran over to Jonah, who,
however, merely raised his hand and said, grandly, "In this
temple, anyone may worship God in his own way."

Perhaps the story of Jonah's mission to the immigrants
can be told best by reprinting the following memoir from
the *Jewish Daily Forward:*

Saturday, February 28, 1959

About fifty years ago in 1909, in my wandering about the
States, I landed in Portland, Oregon. I was looking for work in a
building which was still being constructed, and a piece of wood
fell down on my head. I woke up in a Portland hospital. A few
days later there came to my bed a charming young man who
told me that his name was Jonah Wise and that he was Rabbi of
Temple Beth Israel.

Since at that time I was one of those people who were quite
agnostic, I said that I could find my way to the other world without the guidance of a Rabbi.

"The hospital people telephoned me," the Rabbi continued,
"and they said there was a sick young man in the hospital without any acquaintances and, since that young man said he was
Jewish, they asked me to come. If you had been a Catholic or a
Protestant you would have been visited by representatives of those
particular faiths; and besides," smiled the Rabbi, "I can see that
you're too young at this moment to go to any other world, let alone
Paradise."

After that Dr. Wise came to visit me every day. I told him
about my life and why I was wandering around—how I had left
New York, with its tenements and sweatshops where it was so
difficult for me to breathe—and I told him that I was fancy-free
and like a bird just flying around. Rabbi Wise advised me to
stop wandering and remain in Portland. He said when I left the
hospital to come visit him in the Temple. He would like to invite
me to his home, he said, but he was not married and lived in a
hotel room himself.

I looked around in Portland and I liked it. I became acquainted with other people in my own category and with some
older people and residents of Portland who seemed to have the
same general outlook on life that I had. So we decided to establish
a little organization and develop some of our ideas. When you're
still young and you've got energy it doesn't take long to realize a
decision. So we hired a big room in a Jewish home and, since
literature was then stylish, we gave ourselves a name, *The Jewish
Literary Association of Portland.* Our main objective was to create
a Jewish library. A Jewish doctor became interested in our group.
His wife, a former teacher, became even more interested, and she
became a kind of a matron for our organization. Three nights a
week she used to teach us English, and she arranged the various
courses and lectures.

However, our means were too limited to embark on too
ambitious a course. I told my friends about that young Rabbi
from the German-Jewish Temple and said that he was a very
pleasant man who had a lot of wisdom. "Perhaps we ought to go
to him," I suggested, "and let him speak to us—in English,
naturally." One of the group said, "What—a Rabbi—who needs
them?"

After a little discussion it was decided, however, that two of
us would visit Dr. Wise. Dr. Wise recognized me and he seemed
to be very happy that I remained in Portland. And when he heard
about our suggestion and our idea, his first words were, "I am
very proud of you boys. Why didn't you come to me earlier?"
He continued, and said, "You know, not so long ago we created
in Portland a neighborhood house for Jewish cultural purposes.

They could use a group like yours. They have lovely rooms there. Why don't you see if you could get your group to meet there?"

We explained to the Rabbi that we would like to remain in our little place and not be guided by any other groups or organizations. "That beautiful, lovely neighborhood house," we said, "is not for us."

Wise, however, influenced the neighborhood house to extend an invitation to us to occupy one of their club rooms, which had its own entrance and a certain degree of privacy. He also persuaded the neighborhood house to allow the use of the gym as a lecture hall where we were able to bring large audiences to our meetings. Dr. Wise in actuality became our guide and counselor. He once said to us that he learned much, from becoming acquainted with us, about our manner of life and outlook, and that things seemed a lot clearer to him as a result of his familiarity with us.

In his own lectures he managed to touch upon neither politics nor religion. Abraham Lincoln was his favorite theme. I remember on a Friday night I went to his Temple to talk to him about something; and, since it was near the time for the worship service, he said, "If you have the time and patience, why don't you stay for the service?" "Doctor," I said to him afterwards, "when I heard you preach it seemed to me that you are very versatile; you conduct yourself so well in various situations." "No, no, no," Dr. Wise said. "I am merely interested in every group and do what I can to be of service to all of them."

The 27-year-old Rabbi Wise said that we immigrants gave him the opportunity to understand a corner of Jewish life which up to that time had been completely unknown to him.

Therefore, the news of his death brought me personal sorrow and also stimulated this reminiscence of what happened between us fifty years ago.

> M. Smith
> Paterson, N.J.

If Jonah was living alone in a hotel room when he befriended Mr. Smith, he was not to do so for long. On January 31, 1908, after two years of courtship, he proposed marriage to Helen Rosenfeld, a Portland beauty, and she accepted him. During those two years, or at least a good part of them, Jonah had been an object of relentless pursuit himself. A small army of Portland maidens, with a simpler, more direct, and more vigorous approach than any he had encountered in Chattanooga or his native Cincinnati, had gone into action. An eligible bachelor had appeared on the scene—young, well-placed, well-favored, interesting, attractive to women, endowed with a strong personality and exciting new views —and open season had been declared. Jonah had immediately been thrown on guard. As we have seen, he was ready to settle down at the time of his move to Portland, but he had every intention of singling out his life partner by his own choice. Three times he wrote to himself in his diary, "Watch out, Dodie!"

Helen Rosenfeld was not one of his pursuers. She was still in school when Jonah met her, and was a member of the Altar Guild, an organization of young women who kept the temple sanctuary decorated with fresh flowers. Tall and slim, she rode a horse well and played tennis and golf with more than ordinary skill. In addition, she was an accomplished pianist—although reluctant to perform in public— and had a lively interest in music and the theater.

Even by pre-World War I standards, Helen had been sheltered. Her mother, a former schoolteacher, was shocked when Helen and Jonah took an unchaperoned stroll in the park in broad daylight. Approval was not forthcoming, either, when Jonah took Helen to socialist and suffragist meetings. Furthermore, Jonah's calling of rabbi, although eminently respectable, seemed a little unusual to the Rosenfelds for a man born in the United States. Portland had

never known an American-born rabbi before. The Rosenfelds were distributors of candy and tobacco; two of their
four sons were medical students at Johns Hopkins. Business,
law, medicine—these were the accepted occupations. The
quip with which Jonah summed up this half-suppressed
feeling of theirs has been attributed, in the past half-centu-
ry, to a goodly number of spurious sources. "A rabbi!" he
said. "What kind of job is that for a Jewish boy?" In Cincinnati, the capital of Reform Judaism in America, it had
been job enough, and the high officers of Hebrew Union
College had been among the city's leading citizens.

In view of Jonah's advanced opinions and unconven-
tional occupation, the Rosenfelds sent Helen to New York
for the year 1907–1908 to determine whether her growing
attachment for Jonah was a passing fancy. In New York,
she attended the Benjamin Deane School at 86th Street and
Riverside Drive. Well-bred young ladies came to the Deane
School from all over the country to acquire a final touch of
polish. Helen had a happy year attending concerts and
plays, studying art history, and extending her mastery of
the piano. She returned to Portland with her attachment
to Jonah unweakened.

Jonah and Helen were married in the temple on June
23, 1909. Max Merritt, then rabbi in Evansville, Indiana,
and Eugene Mannheimer, rabbi in Des Moines, crossed the
country to be there. Merritt performed the ceremony and
Mannheimer was the best man.

At first the couple lived in a five-room apartment on
Davis Street. Two children were born there, David in 1910,
Elsa in 1912. Elsa's birth necessitated a further move, this
time to a house in Portland Heights, on 466 South 19th
Street. The infant was carried from the old apartment to

the new house in an apple box—this was highly appropriate to Oregon, a state abounding in apple orchards. A third child, Joan, was born in 1916.

The Wises were a devoted pair, happy in their home life. Jonah, like Isaac Mayer Wise before him, was a sympathetic and indulgent father. The children turned to him as much as to their mother whenever they were sick or had problems. His home was an island of peace to Jonah; he tried to keep it free from the pressures and distractions of the outside world. Politics and religion were not forbidden subjects, but were never discussed; they were left for the forum and the pulpit. Helen Wise reigned over her household with dignity and grace, but it is not recorded that, after marriage, she ever attended another suffragist meeting.

Taking as his example the man in the White House—the first Roosevelt, not the second—Jonah endeared himself to the younger men and women of his flock by stripping away the wall of sanctity that they had been accustomed to find separating rabbis and ordinary people. The great Theodore, whom Jonah greatly admired, was an exponent of "the strenuous life." He set a personal example of physical fitness to a nation that he urged to be physically fit. On occasion, he would invite members of the diplomatic corps and other dignitaries to a presidential breakfast. If they did not know what to expect, they arrived at the White House early in the morning, resplendently attired, to find a sweat-shirted President waiting for them with his four sweat-shirted sons. There would ensue a game of follow-the-leader, with the youngest member of the party as the leader. Breakfast would be served to the winded and rumpled diplomats only after a fast and rugged romp across country, followed by a plunge into the waters of the Potomac. This was Americanism in its purest strain during the first decade of our century.

Jonah was no impetuous Roosevelt; but he was young, he was a first-class athlete and his blood ran swift and high. Outdoor life is a second religion with Oregonians and Jonah joined the natives at its altar. Portland is magnificently located at the meeting of the Willamette and Columbia rivers. The wooded banks of the Willamette rise to impressive heights, and Mt. Hood is fifty miles away. Only minutes from the city there are mountain trails, pine forests, fishing streams, and surf beaches. Jonah fished, swam, picnicked, and rode horseback with members of his congregation. Regularly, on Sunday nights, he played pinochle for small stakes with Milton Kahn, Roscoe Nelson, Ed Neustadter, Ed Frohman, and Arnold Blitz. He became as enthusiastic a gardener as any Oregonian. In time he was a golfer, shooting in the seventies and amassing a cabinetful of cups and trophies. He was a charter member of the Tualatin Country Club, whose velvety greens owed their smoothness of texture to his many years of service as chairman of the greens committee. In his capacity as greens chairman, he introduced a particularly tenacious variety of grass seed from Germany. His excursions into rougher country than golf courses involved an occasional encounter with bears. These meetings were disconcerting, at first, but he soon learned that the bears were no more anxious than he to pursue the acquaintance, and he took their occasional appearances in stride. Mark Warren, proprietor of a summer hotel on Cannon Beach, seventy miles west of Portland, was one of his good friends. The two men spent many days tramping through the thick woods, fishing rod in hand.

There was no road around the beach in those days, and cars had to drive along the beach itself—a dangerous business, in view of the high tides and the speed with which they came roaring in. On many an occasion, the rabbi and the backwoodsman would pile into an old jalopy, rush down to the sand, and rescue a car in immediate danger of being swept into the Pacific.

These activities in no wise corresponded to the community's inherited picture of men of the cloth. Some older eyebrows were raised, but the "sports-model rabbi"—as Felix Warburg affectionately labeled him in later years—discharged his obligations as pastor, educator, and civic leader with equal dedication and elan. Whatever he did, in fact, he gave everything he had. Old and young swiftly realized that they had acquired a spiritual leader who was not only worthy to succeed Stephen S. Wise but was very much a figure of genuine importance in his own right. In spite of his radical connections, he gave them fewer uneasy moments than had Stephen Wise, who had been something of an *enfant terrible*. As Jonah stayed, their pride and affection increased; and when he left, after nineteen years in Portland, the whole community almost literally went into mourning.

Sunday morning services in the early years of the century were already a feature of Reform Jewish congregational life in a few Eastern and Midwestern communities, and, clearly enough, had developed in response to the then universal Monday-through-Saturday business and working week to which the long-established Jews had accommodated themselves. For this very reason, however, it appeared to many a step toward supplanting the traditional Saturday sabbath by the Sunday sabbath of Christianity. Although

no objection to Sunday services could be based on traditional Jewish law—Jews are obliged to pray, congregation-
ally if possible, three times daily—loud outcries were raised
that the holiest inheritance of the Jewish faith was being
subverted. Opinion was so sharply divided and emotions
were so deeply involved that the Central Conference of
American Rabbis forbore to make a concerted determination of this issue, leaving the decision to individual congregations.

Before Jonah's arrival in Portland, Stephen S. Wise had
experimented with Sunday morning lectures in the temple.
These had been delivered to waiting parents who had
brought their children to Sunday school. Jonah instituted
Sunday religious services as a regular feature. He called
them "assemblies" and limited their scope to a carefully
chosen musical program—under him Beth Israel became
famous for its music—and an address by the rabbi. Thus,
he made it clear that he was not providing a substitute for
the regular Sabbath service. The regular Sabbath service,
in accordance with a liturgical tradition nearly two thousand years old, consisted, in addition, of prayers by the
congregation and the reading of the appropriate portion of
the Torah.

There were whispers that the service was short because
Jonah was eager to be off to the Tualatin Country Club.
Underneath his voluminous ministerial robes, it was said,
he wore golf knickers, so that he could reach the first tee
ready to play as soon as possible. Such a practice, if followed, would as likely have endeared him to outdoor-loving
Oregonians as displeased them. There was no truth in the
rumor, nevertheless—or only poetic truth. Jonah was the
most fastidious of men; he always changed his clothes in the

locker room before going on the golf course and after coming off.

The assemblies were well attended, for they had a
strong appeal to many of Portland's Jews who, for whatever
reason, could not attend divine worship on Saturday.
Without the assemblies, those persons would have had no
real contact with synagogue or temple. The Orthodox rabbinate was outraged by the development of Sunday worship. Nehemia Mosessohn, rabbi of Congregation Neveh
Zedek, attacked Jonah savagely in the *Jewish Tribune*. The
attacks were not at all softened by Jonah's willingness to
perform a wedding ceremony over mixed marriages, which
he did partly on compassionate grounds, partly out of concern that partners of different faiths not be lost altogether
to organized religion.

Jonah once performed a funeral over a non-Jew, in
compliance with a wish expressed in the man's will. As
the funeral party turned from the graveside, Jonah asked
the widow of the deceased, "How is it that John, an Episcopalian, wanted a Jewish rabbi to conduct this service?" "He
wasn't a real Episcopalian," she replied, "and you're not a
real rabbi." A real rabbi, presumably, wore a beard. Jonah
told this story over and over. In his desire not to appear
solemn or sentimental or self-important, he persistently
told stories or made remarks that put him in an unfavor-
able or comic light. He would deprecate himself, hiding his
light under a bushel when it was important that it be revealed. In so doing, he not infrequently gave pain to those
who loved and admired him. His sharp tongue, a powerful
weapon with which he deflated the pompous, was double-
edged.

Mosessohn's *Jewish Tribune*, with its editor, moved to

New York, and printed attacks on Jonah from Jewish sources came to an end. When another Jewish publication appeared in Portland, Jonah would be the editor.

Jonah was an outspoken pacifist from the outbreak of the war in Europe in 1914 until the entry of the United States three years later. He was an even more outspoken critic of saber-rattling, war talk, and nationalist ranting in the United States. Although it was suggested by some that he had a soft spot for Germany and the Germans, there is not a scrap of evidence to indicate that his pacifist convictions were based on anything other than commitment to the ideal of peace for all mankind. Universal peace, a central theme of the prophets of Israel, to whose pure form of religion Reform Judaism avowedly returns, is taken seriously by persons who take Reform Judaism seriously. Men of religion often give us offense by putting their religion ahead of the passions of the throng. Certainly, Jonah had great respect for the Germany of Goethe and Schiller and was devoted to Wagnerian opera. He never had any illusions, however, about the cancerous depths of antisemitism in Germany. His cultural allegiance was Anglo-American first of all—to Shakespeare, Walt Whitman, and Mark Twain.

Sympathies on the West Coast were predominantly on the side of the Allied powers, England, France, and Russia. With the unfolding of the great struggle, tempers rose high and partisanship was expressed with growing extravagance. More than ever, Jonah became emotionally involved in the cause of war prevention. He was never afraid, and continued to speak his mind, not just freely but with a bitterness and sarcasm that almost drew blood.

On at least one occasion, the way in which he couched his remarks involved him in a public squabble with the

Portland *Oregonian*. The Kingdom of Italy entered the war on the side of England and France on May 24, 1915, turning against her former allies Austria and Germany in exchange for being promised the territories of Istria and Tyrol upon the war's conclusion. In those innocent days, so naked and reckless an act of political cynicism was still capable of producing a spontaneous outburst of patriotic enthusiasm on the part of its chief victims—the people who would have to do the fighting and dying. The fervor of Italians in the fatherland was transferred to the immigrant Italians in the New World. Italy's entrance into the war occurred a bare two weeks after a German submarine had sunk the Cunard liner *Lusitania*, with heavy loss of life among the many hundreds of neutral Americans aboard. Thus, that year, the observance of Memorial Day—traditionally devoted to remembrance of 1,200,000 Civil War dead—turned into an oratorical free-for-all in which native American wrath coincided with Italian-American nationalistic exuberance and on which the *Oregonian* reported with high approval. Jonah returned from a short vacation and penned a letter at white heat:

Portland, June 1

To the Editor—

Decoration Day is such a fine holiday that I dislike marring it with a note that may spoil the harmony. Upon returning from a fishing trip, with no fish, I found your valued paper to hand and perused it with my usual solicitous curiosity. Amongst the details of maimed, marred and miserable, I found and read extracts from some Decoration Day declamations.

During my piscatorial peregrinations I was at peace. Barring the annoyances of bramble scratches, underdone fried potatoes, cold sleeping quarters, gnats, mosquitoes and such trifles I had repose but no fish. Imagine my annoyance at returning from the humble repose of ichthyological if not theological isolation to find that my fellow civilized citizens had been having an unusually flamboyant scalp dance.

It seems to me that all that rot about fighting and standing behind the President makes poor decorative material. How a crowd of sane men and women can listen to such a fraudulent and spurious set of platitudes is more than I can understand. The burden of the orators was that America is in a critical political situation. What a facetious but blatant lie! People should not joke about serious matters. Look at the horrible example Italy has set us. The Italian people was bedeviled into a bellicose attitude by cheap orators and by apostles of piffle, like D'Annunzio, who is a poet and wants to see humanity with its entrails exposed like Homer did. The Italians were told their national honor demanded war, especially now that it looks like war will pay in more property. That is a low and cheap lie in Italy as it is in America. The National honor demands justice in man and woman, the right to life, liberty and the pursuit of happiness, the privilege of honest work, the prospect of working the soil in one's own name, the abolition of poverty and economic slavery. Aside from that there is no National honor any more than there is a National shoulder to knock chips off. Italy is the home of poverty, illiteracy, organized banditti, and the greatest exporter of excess humanity in the world. A drunken bum who is insulted if you will not drink with him has the same sense of honor as a nation, boozy with poverty, ignorance and excess human garbage; excepting the fact that a drunken bum will not steal, he is profanely and vociferously a person of unsullied virtue, an alcoholically purified Sir Galahad—but a nation is not so particular. While its neighbor is fighting robbers in front, your nation alongside steals your back yard.

Italy was not only brought into war but also to the act of land stealing by just such twaddle as our newspapers and grave ornamenters are pouring out. War produces some heroes, persons who haven't an alert sensibility to bullets or shrapnel. Personally, I have no such immunity. I do not feel that I could benefit my country by having my bowels torn out by a jagged shell. I have met scores of war heroes, I honor the dead, mainly because they are so, but I value none of the pathetic putrescence that war is at all capable of compensating a people by producing a generation of one-legged, blind, deaf, idiotic, and generally maimed heroes for the unfortunate production, alongside these desiderata, of war bastards, murdered women, debauched girls, supply contractors, burned towns, idiot children, bounty jumpers and all the mess and welter that goes with it.

National honor is a matter of the Nation's efficiency in providing opportunity for its citizens. Our newspapers and orators should tell us that and smother these cheap heroics with real patriotism and a distinctive Americanism. Not peace at any price, but peace is the only price. You can't buy honor, prosperity, happiness or virtue with hatred, murder, rape, arson, and robbery, but you can with work, honesty, thrift and self-sacrifice. America is the land of the latter, not the former; the land not of war but peace. I expect to go fishing again on the Fourth of July. What a prospect!

Jonah B. Wise

It is plain from this letter alone how far, in less than a year of war abroad, discussion of the war had departed from the usages of polite discourse. The *Oregonian* answered Jonah with less sarcasm but just as angrily:

Rabbi Wise's flippant comments on Memorial Day do no credit to his judgment. When his friends read his letter in the Oregonian today it will not surprise us if they wish he had stayed on his trip until his sophomoric effervescence found some other outlet. Rabbi Wise lives in a country of free speech and he is therefore permitted to refer to one of our great National holidays as "an unusually flamboyant scalp dance." He may call our loyalty to the President and the ideals of the country "rot," and speak of its expression as "a fraudulent and spurious set of platitudes." The conviction that the country is in a critical political condition he may say "is a blatant lie." The liberty to insult the

American people is part of that heritage of freedom which the American people have won and presented to all who choose to live here. Rabbi Wise may, without any personal danger, ridicule and despise the reverence we feel for the heroes of the great struggles that bought this privilege. If he lived in some other countries, particularly one that he seems greatly to admire, his conduct would hardly be dealt with so mildly.

When Rabbi Wise is older and less puffed up with the conceit of infallibility, he will probably regret his unwarranted sneers at Italy and the Italians. The young lady graduate who wondered that "one head could contain all she knew" might envy the extent of his apparent ignorance concerning that country. To Rabbi Wise, Italy is "the home of poverty, illiteracy and organized banditti." To all who know the rudiments of current history it is the land of intelligent cooperation, of wonderful advances in popular education and of high national ideals. If its people have gone into the war without just cause, we could easily name others who have done the same, though they have not provoked Rabbi Wise's ire. He takes in his letter the stand of a thoroughgoing materialist. We do not blame him for this. It is his right if he wishes to do so. We merely wonder at it a little. National honor as he conceives it consists of physical comfort, and nothing more. As long as the people are permitted by their conquerors to devour their daily portion of "pigwash," as Carlyle called it, they need not care what else happens to them. Rabbi Wise does not appear to see anything regrettable in the spiritual death of a nation, the ruin of its ideals, and the destruction of the soul life. The main thing is to avoid war and its horrors, which seem to appeal to Rabbi Wise with singular force. It may not be out of place to remind him that men as good and bright as he is have endured all those horrors without shrinking, for the sake of the ideals they held dearer than life. It is no particular credit to a man that he prefers his own safety to everything else in the world.

What is a nation to do when it is attacked and theatened with the horrors of invasion? Shall it lie down and beg mercy from the invader? When a monarch goes on the warpath for what he can make out of fighting, is he likely to be moved by pleas of

mercy? Will such pleas stay him from "destroying all the intellectual and moral resources of the conquered"? We confess frankly
that, in our opinion, when a war party makes itself the common
foe of mankind and threatens the civilization of the world with
ruin, the only wise and safe course is to extirpate it as we would
extirpate a den of ravening wolves. Nobody but a hopeless fool
would try to make peace with a rattlesnake or a mad dog. It is
recorded that St. Francis preached to the birds, but we do not
learn that he converted any vultures from their old habit of
murdering doves. Rabbi Wise might have better luck but we
doubt it.

It is not difficult, from his reply to this acrimonious
editorial, to deduce that Jonah realized that his derisiveness
had been ill-advised. On the other hand, he stuck to his
guns. The result was an effective statement of his position:

Portland, June 3

To the Editor—

Your editorial comment put the worst possible construction
on my letter. In reading the letter I find some of the errors to
which you refer, but they arise from your construction, not my
intent. Had you wished, I believe that you could have read my
purpose more kindly. I am willing to admit that a man should
never joke in the presence of profound and self-conscious loyalty
such as yours, except about the weather, as you do, and I apolo-
gize. I laid myself open to attack, but not from a source inclined
to be friendly, and I therefore feel that a statement from me as to
my construction of my letter is but simple justice to myself.

I may be sophomoric and cowardly as well as all the things
you are not, but I am not lacking in respect for the true ideal of
Decoration Day. What I do wish to call attention to is the distinction we should make between the sincere celebration of the day
and the base uses to which it is put. I refer distinctly and clearly

to that species of war talk which I think is insincere and dangerous. The hands of President Wilson are not upheld by those who shout to him that the Nation is ready to fight. He is embarrassed by those champions in his efforts which are distinctly for peace and not for war. Militarists have called peace talk twaddle and gush. Personally I believe now, as I did before I read that I was a coward and all that, that war talk is the veriest gush and those who talk it cannot be sincere.

Ninety-nine per cent of the men who go to war hate it and despise it. Ask the veterans of the Civil War, and they will tell you that emphatically. The men who were spiritually so animated that they offered their lives for this country are the very ones who despise this vainglory and understand the horror and the coward-ice of what you praise.

The appetite for war with Spain was stimulated in this coun-try, nay created (I use the term "created" advisedly) by the irre-sponsible press at the instigation of piratical interests. Spain had yielded every point, had given every concession we fought for, and yet we attacked Spain. I say it again, "We attacked Spain." A low press and thoughtless mouthers about patriotism killed off those brave men and boys whose memory ought to be a warning when we celebrate it properly.

I have lived in Italy. You may be very cheerful about its pro-gress and the happiness it brings to its citizens. Do you know that the Mafia and Black Hand do not spring from Italian perverseness, but from poverty, ignorance and songs about arms? Italy has made wonderful strides, but that is just the horror of it. A nation so capable of self-help, seemingly so willing to meet the obliga-tions of the state to the citizens (purely material if you choose) is a sad spectacle when one sees it dragged down from that high enterprise to the level of cheap politicians, who send it to war that means crippling its better life for years. Nothing you can say will move me from the conviction that Italy needs peace and that war, not Austria, is its worst enemy.

Italy has a large Socialist party, as have Germany, France, Belgium, and Austria. Please do not shut your eyes to the facts, do not be willfully blind. You know that these parties yielded to the cry for war reluctantly. They see eye to eye with other thinkers that war is produced by the classes, not the masses. I quote from Half Century Ago column of today:

"The wealthier classes of the South, who plunged this country into the horrors of the Civil War, are now feeling the truth and force of the old adage, 'Sorrow tracketh crime.' "

Plainly the editor of that day was a wise man. He saw the reality of war, not its tinsel.

One of the reasons I felt and expressed myself so bitterly, aside from my well-known cowardice, is that I am personally in receipt of information about the present results of this war that are so revolting as to make me feel that peace cannot be too dearly bought. Aside from the death of thousands every day, to which we are so readily reconciled, aside from the horror of the Lusitania affair, which is public, I trust you are informed of the fact that in every city in Europe the asylums for idiots are being crowded and new ones built. You add to these the number that lunacy has sent, hopeless but harmless, to the other ones to drag out a life of such pain that no man can touch its outer shell and be unmoved. You are no doubt informed of the number of girls raped in England by their own soldiers. You may not be informed as my source, private though reliable, that the number of suicides of pregnant girls in Galicia is unbelievable. I have news as to Belgium. I am sure you do, also. Blind schools are springing up all over Europe, and charity is serving those whom patriotism has blinded. This is aside from the dead, wounded and missing. Half Europe will be maimed, shamed, groping, dead, or demented. It takes a brave man to pull his little children into this sort of thing.

I made the error of joking at the beginning of my letter, but I was in earnest at the end. Whatever you think about the sophomoric heroics of it, I still think that peace is the only price. The courage, self-sacrifice, vision, energy and patriotism which feeds men to Mars can so feed humanity that it will save humanity.

You are rancorous about what you suggest is my pro-German attitude. I am pro-America, and you are allowing your hatred for Germany to teach you that we should sacrifice our country upon the bloody altar of European feuds. You do not know Europe, or you would love America so that you would gladly sever it from the hot welter of racial and national animosities.

We have no point of contact with European politics that can remotely suggest war. I fear war as an entanglement with European chaos and hatreds. Therefore I am shocked and grieved when I hear the present situation described as a crisis. I was born in Ohio, yet I know how the foreign-born man and woman dread the thing you love, and pray not for peace alone but for the fulfillment of America's ideal as a land where the white man can work out his salvation, detached from the shackles of ancestral feuds. When war is declared this sort of man will stand forth first, for he knows.

My personal suffering from your scurrilous attack I can bear with equanimity, for I feel that it enables me to bring before a large public that part of the ideal which humanity finds unique in American life. Peace is the price we must pay for human happiness. Ancient Israel describes the Messiah as a Prince of Peace, but despised and rejected of men. You will find those who struggle for the salvation of men through the messianic ideal not always ready to speak the whole truth, and the truth alone can free. You are a Christian, I am not. You know that well; therefore I can leave the preaching of peace to you.

Jonah B. Wise

Jonah's "private source" was the *Israelite*, which subscribed to the Jewish Telegraphic Agency wire service and, in addition, had special correspondents in the warring countries.

The *Oregonian* was, on the whole, conciliatory in its rejoinder to Jonah's reply. It denied insinuating that Jonah was a coward, "for he gives proof that he is a very bold man." Even as it reasserted its belief that America was being endangered by Germany's activities, it had no stomach for continuing the controversy, and announced that publication of letters on the topic would close. Jonah's efforts persisted; and he had the satisfaction of receiving praise for them in the very columns in which he had been attacked. This in March, 1917, a bare month before the United States declared war.

The Beth Israel congregation neither opposed Jonah nor backed him up in his pacifist activities, for it was as divided on the question as the nation and the community. On the very day of the inflammatory speechmaking that aroused his ire, his contract was renewed for three years at $6000 a year, a respectable income for those days and the equivalent of much more today—especially after taxes. Jonah's right to speak his mind was never in question.

A word of explanation may be in order about Jonah's reference, in his second letter, to "America's ideal as a land where the white man can work out his salvation." It would be incorrect to construe this remark as indicating prejudice toward men of color. On the contrary, its source was recognition of America's historic injustice toward Negroes, Indians, and Orientals. Throughout the first three years of the conflict, he denounced race pride as "the most hideous fetich of our time." It was, he said, "the spark that exploded the present war." On the same Memorial Day whose manner of celebration touched off his anger, he wrote for the *Oregonian*:

The white race has, since time was young, considered itself peculiarly fitted to rule the world. The lighter the color of the human being, the bluer his eyes, and the blonder his hair the more he argues himself a dominant individual....This will to mastery is part of the white man's burden....One of the sacred privileges of a white skin is to plunder all persons of black, brown, red and yellow colors....The white nations cannot live at peace with their neighbors....The ideal of peace cannot even be mentioned as a part of the political ideas of Caucasian society.

And he went on to remark that the difference between the two major powers contending in the war was that Germany was candid in her racialism and England ashamed of it.

War came to America in April, 1917. President Wilson proclaimed the war a crusade for universal peace, and it was so accepted by the American people, Jonah among them. Jonah did everything and more that could be asked of a community leader. Teamed with his old partner in philanthropy and fund raising, Ben Selling, former lieutenant governor of Oregon, he sold Liberty Bonds and raised large sums for the Red Cross.

Insofar as he was able, Jonah continued to stand for freedom of speech and thought in the midst of pressures to close ranks and make all reluctant or dissident elements toe the line. For example, in Portland as elsewhere, compliance with Liberty Loan drives came very close to being forced. Children in the schools were asked to stand up at their desks and report how many Liberty Bonds had been purchased by their families. Organizations canvassed their staffs and made weekly contributions to financial drives obligatory. The public library, in conducting such a canvass, met with opposition from a librarian, Miss Louise Hunt, who, on conscientious grounds, refused to purchase bonds. Miss Hunt, accordingly, was brought up on charges before the board of trustees of the Portland Library Association, with her job at stake. Insisting upon the right of anyone to his opinion, so long as it was not directed actively against public policy, Jonah persuaded his fellow directors that it was important not to lose sight of what was meant when it was said, "We are fighting to save the world for democracy." Accordingly, cool heads prevailed, and Miss Hunt kept her job. "So long as I know that such sentiments are held by people of eminence in our community," an admirer wrote Jonah, "I shall less regret the necessary curtailment of civil liberty, the sacrifices always a part of war, and confidently realize that with the return of peace will come a liberty more complete than ever." During the Red Scare of 1920-21, Jonah remained a stanch advocate of civil liberty. He had understanding for the hated and reviled IWWS of the lumber camps, even though he disagreed with their views. He resolutely set himself against the surging spirit of violence that followed the war in a kind of rhythmic reaction, and once again took a lonely position on the West Coast when he denounced the savage riots at Centralia and Walla Walla.

Jonah's activities in Jewish war relief were, ultimately, to change his life. The great battles between Russia and Germany in 1915 and 1916 swept back and forth across the Jewish settlements in Poland, Galicia, the Ukraine, and Romania. Whatever disasters befell the gentile population of those lands were ten times multiplied for the Jews. The Russians with callous brutality deported 500,000 of them in the first year of the war. Seven years more of wars, revolution, and famine added 6,000,000 more Jews to the ranks of the naked and starving. The Joint Distribution Committee, under the leadership of Felix Warburg, Louis Marshall, Henry Morgenthau, Jacob Schiff, and Julius Rosenwald, was formed in 1915 to deal with this appalling crisis, using funds raised by Morgenthau's Campaign for Jewish War Relief. Jonah and Ben Selling spearheaded the West Coast drive, raising sums that no one in the area had ever believed possible. In consequence, they became national figures in the realm of Jewish philanthropy; and there can be little doubt that this success in raising money for Jewish causes was instrumental in Jonah's later selection, first as Rabbi of Central Synagogue, New York, and, second, as chairman of the Joint Distribution Committee.

Jonah's wide social interests and outstanding record in social service continued to bring him appointments to state boards and commissions—milk, higher education, conservation, and so on. When the Portland Social Hygiene Committee was set up, Jonah was made a member. The committee received a large subvention from the State of Oregon, and carried on an active campaign for the prevention and treatment of venereal disease. A new arrival in Portland, an Episcopalian bishop, Bishop Sumner, was also made a member of the committee. In Chicago Bishop Sumner had belonged to the Committee of One Hundred, whose exhaustive report on conditions in that city had led to the banning of commercial prostitution. The full membership of the Social Hygiene Committee was asked to be present on the day that the bishop was to put in his first appearance and accept membership. When all the members had been introduced, the committee chairman turned to the newcomer and said, "Bishop Sumner, we are familiar with your accomplishments in Chicago, and would appreciate your touching on some of the highlights of your work in the Committee of One Hundred."

"First," said the bishop, "let me hear about your local program."

The chairman proceeded to tell him that the Portland

committee was advertising in local newspapers, putting up signs in rest rooms, and publicizing treatment centers. He finished by saying, "And we have followed the example of your campaign in Chicago. We have secured legislation that outlaws brothels in Portland."

"Excellent! Excellent!" cried the bishop. "But not enough! Not enough!

"To legislate brothels out of existence is the first step. But do you have a follow-up system? We had one in Chicago. We followed prostitutes when they infiltrated residential districts. We publicized their presence, and that did the job.

"Ladies and gentlemen," he went on, "I became so familiar with the ways of those prostitutes trying to set up their establishments all over again that I could smell them out."

"What a talent!" commented Jonah. "And wasted on a bishop!" The session broke up in a roar of laughter.

Jonah's irreverent humor kept committee work from becoming tiresome, and added to his popularity. However —although instances have been cited—he rarely allowed it to undermine his serious social service or religious work.

In the 1920s, Jonah knew the deep satisfaction of seeing his work among the Orthodox come to a great flowering. One after another, sons of the Orthodox who had come under his influence elected to study for the Reform ministry. Some of them Jonah sponsored actively, recommending a rabbinical career as matching their talents and as tending to strengthen the body of Reform. Others became interested through observing his example and following it. It may be said that he had no such influence on the younger members of his own congregation, in spite of his great popularity with

them. The sons of Reform did not become rabbis; and
Jonah, if he was able to preserve their close, harmonious
connection with organized religion, was well satisfied.

Among the young men of Portland who went to Hebrew
Union College in Cincinnati or to the newly formed Jewish
Institute of Religion in New York to become Reform rabbis
were Harold Reinhardt, now of London, England; Alvin
Fine of San Francisco; Lewis Browne, now deceased, who
left the rabbinate for a literary career; Max Maccaby, also
deceased, of Mt. Vernon, N.Y.; Samuel Gordon of Rye,
N. Y.; and Jacob J. Weinstein of KAM Temple, in Chicago. Jonah took a personal interest in those young men; he
was no recruiting sergeant. They were his boys as well as
younger colleagues and friends. He looked out for them. He
got the Sisterhood of his temple to provide them with schol-
arships. When they were away at the seminary he followed
their careers and made frequent visits to their families back
home to report on their progress. When they were in Portland he called upon them for assistance in running the
temple. Still another young protégé, Jacob Weinstein's
brother Sam, a lawyer, joined Beth Israel as a member, and
became its president fifteen years after Jonah left for New
York.

Jonah was alert to the welfare of Hebrew Union College
in still other ways. He took great interest in the growth of
its library, already one of the world's great depositories of
Judaica as well as an efficient working library for the education of seminarists. He learned in 1923 that the unique
Chinese Hebrew manuscript collection of the London
Society for Promoting Christianity among the Jews—com-
prising 59 of the known 63 manuscripts by Jews living in
China—was available for purchase. The society had ac-

quired it from the disintegrating Jewish community of Kae-fung-foo in 1849. The collection included six scrolls of the Law, a sixteenth-century Talmud, and many smaller man-uscripts. Some of them had been translated from the He-brew into the Jewish-Persian dialect, and constituted direct evidence for a relation between Jewish-Persian and Jewish-Chinese rituals. Jonah informed Adolph Oko, the College librarian, of this great opportunity, and Ben Selling, Jonah's inevitable associate in such matters, pledged $5000 as a beginning toward acquiring the Kae-fung-foo collection for HUC. Oko was no less active in Cincinnati, and friends of the College agreed to spend up to $75,000 for this purpose. In March 1924 the transaction was concluded, and those unique documents went to Cincinnati for the very reason-able sum of $50,000.

Jonah not only maintained his own personal and pro-fessional relationships with Jewish groups in the rest of the country; he was also active in keeping Jewish communities in touch with one another. The *Scribe*, a new Jewish weekly, was organized by him in Portland in 1919. It was world-wide in its coverage of news and features, although regional in circulation. Its columns were often filled by contributors with international reputations. One such contributor was Dr. Jacob R. Marcus of Hebrew Union College, now pro-fessor of Jewish history there and director of the American Jewish Archives. Marcus sent the *Scribe* a series of essays on Jewish history. These bore their immense weight of scholar-ship lightly. Their graceful style and popular appeal, as Jonah had foreseen, made them particularly effective brief-ing material for teachers in religious schools. Throughout the Mountain and Northwest area they were put to this useful purpose.

The *Scribe* was published in Portland until 1952, filling the gap left when Nehemia Mosessohn's *Jewish Tribune* was removed to New York in 1918. It was managed by David E. Cohen, who became its editor after Jonah left Portland. The *Scribe* served Oregon, Washington, Idaho, Utah, Montana, Alaska, and British Columbia, a vast area corresponding to District Four of the Union of American Hebrew Congregations. Jonah was president of District Four.

Although the *Scribe* was presumably addressed to every shading of Jew—Orthodox and Reform, Zionist and non-Zionist—and publicized the schedules and programs of all temples and synagogues in the area, its witty, spirited, informed, and unsigned editorials were not always to the liking of Orthodoxy and Conservatism. An article on liturgical music, for example, referred to the traditional chanting of the synagogue as "archaic and too narrowly associated with one tone and one thought. It does not even express the modern Jew. It is a memory; it is a dirge of ghettos, Wailing Walls and wildernesses."

On Saturday evening, December 29, 1923, the Beth Israel temple was destroyed by fire—only two months after a similar loss had been inflicted mysteriously upon the neighboring Conservative synagogue Ahavai Sholom. The arsonist turned out to be a pyromaniac who had joined the Portland Fire Department; the burning of the temple was motivated by illness of the mind, and was not an expression of antisemitic malice.

Jonah was in the crowd that rushed to the scene and made brave efforts to save some of the temple's treasures; but records, scrolls of the Law, Torah crowns and ornaments all went up in the flames. Jonah described the scene in the pages of the *Scribe*:

As the mass of flames leaped at the great wooden towers they seemed alive and like some wild animal expecting an easy prey. Battled, they were thrown off again and again. Firemen, spectators and police expected the towers to fall, yet they wrestled in desperate conflict with the flames and the battering of tons of water thrown against them. And in the end, they came out victorious, blackened and ruined, lame as Israel at the ford of Jabbok; they won their victory for which they had been built, and the wooden towers of the western front, in its own great will to win, stand today, melancholy in their bold exposure to the cold and snow, but victorious.

If ever I was proud of Israel, I was so indeed when I saw the flames tearing at the vitals of its Holy House, and saw that sacred structure, like a sentient being, accept the gage of battle and fight back until it was left a hideous ruin but still standing.

The following account is taken from *The Ties Between,* a history of Congregation Beth Israel written by its rabbi in 1959, Dr. Julius J. Nodel:

No story of *Beth Israel* would be complete without reference to the loyal sexton of The Temple, Theodore A. Olsen, who reached the heights of heroic devotion in the 1923 disaster. At least three generations of *Beth Israel* families had come under the influence of Mr. Olsen during his forty-seven year career as custodian for the Congregation. Although he remained a Christian throughout his ninety years of life, he came to Temple *Beth Israel* as a laborer and left as a legend. On the occasion of his twenty-fifth year with Temple *Beth Israel*, in 1929, a special Service to honor him was held and a resolution of appreciation was adopted by the Congregation: "During this quarter of a century Mr. Olsen has labored conscientiously and devotedly without thought of self. He has given a type of consecrated service which cannot be measured in material terms. Mr. Olsen has become an institution in the life of Congregation *Beth Israel*. His relation to the members is one of mutual respect and affection, and his modesty, his integrity and his noble character have endeared him to the entire community."

At the conclusion of that Service, Olsen gave a speech—the first and only speech he ever delivered in The Temple. It wasn't long, just a few well-chosen words in his rich Norwegian brogue: "I am very proud to be a *shammas*. To be a *shammas* is a great honor. I have tried to do my work with that thought in mind and nobody could be happier than I am to have such a big responsibility."

Though he was not an orator, Olsen was a connoisseur of sermons as well as rabbis. He had put many a rabbi in his place by maintaining a grim silence when the rabbi's sermon was poor. If the sermon was good, Mr. Olsen maintained a pleasant silence; but if Olsen ever said a sermon was good, you knew it was immortal. Rabbis came and rabbis went, but Olsen went on for almost six decades. Men and women today with grandchildren of their own can remember how Olsen used to hurry them to their Sunday School classes and reprimand them for not behaving in The Temple; how he used to climb up into the towers of the old Temple to look for mischievous boys who played hooky by hiding there when they should have been in Hebrew School classes or at Services. Before the Services began, Olsen would open up the *Torah* to the proper passage which the Rabbi was to read. He did not know a word of Hebrew, but he never failed to have the *Torah* turned to the right place. He had developed his own system: he carried in his vest-pocket a Jewish calendar on which was written the Hebrew word opposite each Sabbath morning date, giving the name of the week's Scriptural portion. Olsen used merely to fix his eye on the little word, study its configuration, and proceed to find its counterpart in the *Torah*.

In Spring and Fall, he used to go out to the country, hiring a truck for the purpose, to bring back vast pyramids of green and gold and red flowers and arrange them on The Temple pulpit or construct a *Succo* out of them for the Feast of Tabernacles. One year when Portland was visited by a week of unusually cold weather, Olsen never left The Temple at all but spread a blanket on the floor and slept there at night so that he could keep the fires going and prevent a freeze-up.

On the occasion of his twenty-fifth anniversary the Congregation finally forced him to take his first vacation. Up to that time he had only been absent from work nine days, and that because he had caught a cold. The reason for his constant devotion and attendance was that he could not leave "his Temple" in the hands of "an irreverent substitute." When Olsen finally did take his vacation, the man who stepped into his shoes was so deluged with Olsen's admonitions and instructions that the poor fellow walked around on tiptoe and never spoke above a whisper.

In a small supply room which served as "Olsen's office," he created a little museum of his own about the Congregation's history. Its walls were covered with pictures and newspaper clippings about all the old Rabbis and former Presidents; programs of congregational anniversaries, confirmation classes and bulletins. He used to love to show these treasures to those who came from far and wide to see the Temple, and if he liked you because you spoke well of his Temple, he would, perhaps, give you as a souvenir a picture postcard which he himself had made showing the old Temple and the new Temple side by side. If you were thus favored, you would be grateful, for it was this card that Olsen used to send his Baptist friends for Christmas.

From the time of the great fire, Theodore Olsen became a fabulous figure in the eyes of the community. He was there among the firemen, without a hat, his eyebrows burned off, his face a blackened mask streaked with sweat and tears, his clothes a dishevelled bundle of soaking wet rags; he was a man possessed, blinded with smoke, insane with grief, raving at the fire-fighters, shaking his clenched fist in pitiful gestures of despair as his beloved Temple was consumed by the flames.

But he had not been shocked beyond the use of his reason. He had not sailed the North Sea in vain when, as a boy, he had performed his fearless duties as a sailor in many a savage storm; and in this greatest crisis of all his life, his one thought had been for the *Torahs* that were still enclosed in the Holy Ark, in the very heart of the seething furnace. This story really should end with Olsen fighting his way through the fire to rescue the Sacred Scrolls and to emerge heroically bearing aloft the words that had been born among the fires of *Sinai*. But such would not be fact. What really occurred was far more devastating because of the awful spiritual suffering through which the man passed. He was totally unaware of his wounds; it was his spirit that was broken, his pride, his honor, for he had fought his way up the aisle half the distance only to see a sheet of flame like a bloody fang tear up the curtain before the Ark and devour the *Torah* Scrolls before his tortured gaze. But Olsen was not through. Prayer books were at hand to be seized and salvaged. Out through the door he raced and around to the back to enter the smoke-filled vestry-rooms and carry out whatever books and records he could reach. Whatever he could lay his hands on, in the darkness and smoke, he snatched up and bore out to safety. In the archives of Temple *Beth Israel* are books and papers slightly charred and blistered from water. When we look at them we think of Olsen on that dreadful night when he walked into the valley of the shadow.

Today, the body of Theodore A. Olsen, in accordance with his final request, lies buried in *Beth Israel* Cemetery. His grave lies among the hundreds of men, women and children who knew him and loved him; who were served by him; whose lives were made more exalted whenever they came to their House of God because Olsen had helped to prepare the way for them.

The Portland community's response to the stricken congregation was sympathetic and generous. Beth Israel was offered a temporary home by virtually every church in the city. Friday evening services were held at the First Presbyterian Church. Saturday morning services were held jointly with Ahavai Sholom—also homeless—at the B'nai Brith Center. The religious school was conducted weekday afternoons in a public school building.

The last years of Jonah's ministry in Portland were devoted to the formidable task of raising funds for a new temple building. He began this task himself but left its completion to other hands, for he was called to his new pulpit in New York when the new structure was only half-finished.

The old temple building, a twin-towered 35-year-old neo-Moorish basilica, had been among the showplaces of Portland. A larger and handsomer temple, Byzantine in style and crowned by a massive dome, rose on the corner of Northwest 19th and Flanders Streets. John Bennes and Harry Herzog were the design architects, with Morris Whitehouse and Herman Brookman associated. It was dedicated in a three-day ceremony beginning April 27, 1928. Jonah, who had been so closely involved in its beginnings, was there for the dedication, although a successor, Rabbi Henry Berkowitz, officiated. The scroll of the Law that Rabbi Berkowitz carried to the waiting ark was a donation from New York's Central Synagogue—a graceful gesture to the former home of its spiritual leader.

V

New York

WHEN ISAAC MAYER WISE DIED IN 1900, fewer Americans were city dwellers than villagers and farmers. The small, decentralized, and leisurely United States of wistful memory had not disappeared completely. New York led all other cities in banking and trade, as it had for the better part of a century, but owned nothing approaching a monopoly. Boston and New England still held first place (or so everyone thought) in literature and the politer arts. Chicago, with its architects of genius and their skyscrapers of original design, was the center of masterful architecture. Among its glories was Temple KAM, noblest of all synagogue houses and the work of the great Louis H. Sullivan. Sullivan's partner, Dankmar Adler, was a member of KAM.

When Isaac Mayer Wise's son Jonah went to Portland six years later, he thought that a lifetime of service could be performed as effectively there as anywhere. A new America, however, was already in being. New York was becoming headquarters for almost all major aspects of American life

1   *Silhouette of Isaac Mayer and Theresa Bloch Wise, Albany, 1846.*

2   *Selma Bondi Wise, Jonah Wise's mother, circa 1920.*

3   *Hexter's Hotel, Cincinnati, Jonah Wise's birthplace.*

4   *Isaac Mayer Wise Farmhouse, College Hill, Ohio. Etching in possession
Hebrew Union College–Jewish Institute of Religion, Cincinnati.*

5   *The twins. Jonah and Jean, 1884.*

6 *Jonah's schoolmates at one-room country school in College Hill. Jonah was
late for school when this picture was taken, and he does not appear.*

7 *At the farm with his father, 1899.*

8   *With Max Merritt (left) and Julian Morgenstern, Amsterdam, 1903.*

9   *In student skit, Berlin University, 1903.*

10   *With Max Merritt, Berlin, 1903.*

11   *With Dr. Bloch of Bloch Publishing Company, 1905. Dr. Bloch was a cousin of Theresa Bloch Wise, Isaac Mayer Wise's first wife.*

12   *Portland, 1906.*

13   *Helen Rosenfeld in 1908. Engagement picture of the future Mrs. Jonah Wise.*

14 *Portland, circa 1920.*

15   *On Cannon Beach, Oregon, 1921, with children David, Elsa, and Joan.*

16   *New York, circa 1935.*

17   *In his study at Central Synagogue community house, 1939.*

18   *With Catholic priest (left) and the Reverend Ralph W. Sockman at inter-*
      faith exercises, New York World's Fair Court of Peace, 1940.

19 *Transatlantic broadcasting via short wave.*

20   *With Albert Einstein on the* Message of Israel, *1939.*

21   *With Rabbi Maurice Eisendrath, President of the Union of American Hebrew Congregations, on the* Message of Israel, *1957.*

22 *Three generations of Wises at the cornerstone laying of the new building of
the Union of American Hebrew Congregations on Fifth Avenue at 65th Street,
New York. (Left to right) David, Jonah, and Jonathan.*

23 *How to raise 2 billion dollars: Jonah Wise as one of the speakers at a campaign dinner of the United Jewish Appeal. His seated co-workers are Edward M. M. Warburg and Paul Baerwald.*

RABBI JONAH B. WISE
NEW-YORK

24   *The vice-chairman of the Joint Distribution Committee takes the micro-phone at the JDC's eighth postwar conference, Paris, 1954.*

PHOTO BY JEROME SILBERSTEIN.

25   *Receiving an honorary doctorate from Jewish Theological Seminary, New York, 1949. Other degree recipients included Henry Morgenthau and Paul Baerwald, who stand beside him on the immediate left and right.*

26   *Assisted by Rabbi Seligson* (right), *Cantor Lechner* (bottom left) *and the two Protestant clergymen Dr. Spears and Dr. Sockman, Jonah Wise conducts a union Thanksgiving service at Central Synagogue, 1955.*

27   *After the service. Dr. Ralph Sockman and Dr. Theodore C. Spears beside Jonah Wise.*

28   *With Dr. Maurice Eisendrath, President of the Union of American Hebrew Congregations, at the dedication of a bust of Isaac Mayer Wise in the UAHC's House of Living Judaism. The two men hold a bound copy of* The Israelite, *the English-language Jewish periodical founded by Isaac Mayer Wise.*

29 *Relaxing with grandchildren Sarah Helen Kaufman, aged two, and Anne Wise Herzberg, aged four, at Fircones, his first summer rental home in the country.*

30   *Helen Rosenfeld Wise, just before her death in 1950.*

31   *Pointing out landmark plaque on exterior of Central Synagogue to interested family group. (Bottom row, left to right) Daniel Wise Kaufman, Jonathan Franklin Wise, Jeremy Alan Wise. (Top row) David Wise, Edward Gross, and Jonah Wise.*

32   *The twins. Jonah Wise and Mrs. Jean May, 1955.*

and thought. Its attraction could be felt for thousands of miles, and was starting to drain away the best young talents and abilities from the regions of their birth. A respectable number of Jews contributed to New York's advancing life, but the mass were still submerged in poverty and imperfectly adjusted to the New World.

World War I speeded the concentration of America's important energies in the city of New York. And, in the 1920s, the metropolis grew extravagantly and flowered mightily. The swelling roar of traffic intensified an atmosphere of great excitement. Miles of opulent multistoreyed apartment dwellings rose on both sides of Park Avenue. Massive towers consecrated to big business and high finance sprouted all the way from Central Park to the Battery. New hotels, theaters, fanciful movie palaces, dance halls, and speakeasies gave a festive welcome to a city-sized floating population swarming in daily from every corner of the United States. A spirited intellectual and artistic life challenged the primacy of London, Paris, and Berlin. New York was clearly on its way toward its present position as capital of the world.

It was already the capital of the Jewish world. Nearly two million Jews lived within the city limits—half the Jews of the country, a fourth of New York's total population, an eighth of all the Jews on earth. They were now liberated from poverty; and a generation had matured that knew only America as its home. Jews played their proportionate role in the brisk New York life of the twenties—a disproportionate role, perhaps, in social welfare, medicine, entertainment, and the arts. New York would have been poorer by far without them.

The New York Jewish community's demand for men of

ability to conduct its affairs and participate in its important
work was then, as now, insatiable. It was inevitable that it
would bid for Jonah's services, and inevitable, too, that he
would accept.

In 1923, Nathan Krass, rabbi of New York's Central
Synagogue, went to neighboring Temple Emanu-El. After
that, things did not go well for Central. At first, forces were
joined with Stephen S. Wise's Free Synagogue. Services
were conducted at Central on Friday evenings, Saturday
mornings, and festivals; at Carnegie Hall on Sundays; and
at both places on the High Holy Days. The joint ministry
included an assistant rabbi; even so, Stephen Wise's Sia-
mese-twin congregations were too much for him. He was
heavily engaged with the American Jewish Congress and
with the Jewish Institute of Religion, of which he was not
only founder but president. A new house of worship big
enough to accommodate one consolidated congregation
would have slimmed his work load to manageable propor-
tions. The two boards of trustees, when talking merger, had
agreed ultimately to consolidate. But the need to raise a vast
sum for a new synagogue building came upon them so
quickly that it was deemed wiser to separate. Stephen Wise,
of course, was to remain with the Free Synagogue, his own
child. Meanwhile, Central was losing ground. New members were not being recruited to make up for normal attrition, and the religious school was deteriorating. Unless
President Samuel Hamburger and his board could find a
minister of the highest caliber, Central would be in danger
of becoming a shadow of its former prestigious self.

Jonah was no stranger to Central Synagogue, and he
was known as a man who got things done. He was also the
son of a most distinguished father. When his name came

before the board, Stephen Wise endorsed him warmly. "I have felt for months," he wrote Mr. Hamburger, "that no better man could be found for the post.... He has very much more than a tradition and a great name behind him. He is a man of personal charm, of scholarly habit, of unusual gifts as a writer and of clarity and power as a preacher.... If Rabbi Wise is elected he will come to exercise a wide and significant influence in the life of our great community. I am of the hope that his election will be unanimous...." Jonah was made Central's first choice.

When Central's offer came, he was 44 years old, confident, experienced, at the height of his physical and mental powers—and more than a little restless. Challenges exhilarated him. They provided an outlet for his strong sense of obligation, and fed his driving need to live and grow. Central's urgent need of leadership was a big inducement for him to provide it. So strategic a base as Central, moreover, held a promise of opportunity for translating his deepest convictions into effective action. He had no idea what his opportunities would be, but he knew their season would come. His wife eased his path of decision, and he said yes.

In accepting, Jonah stipulated that he would remain in Portland through 1925 and that Central would assume the burden of his remuneration for the last six months of that year. He did not wish Beth Israel to be hard pressed in its search for his successor. Central's trustees were more than willing to comply.

During his last months on the West Coast, Jonah pulled up, one after another, the deep roots he had put down over the previous nineteen years. They were not easy months. His congregation was shocked and disbelieving. In hopes

that he might be persuaded to remain, it put off filling the
pulpit; this problem was solved when Max Merritt accepted
a caretaker appointment for the period of a year. Although
Jonah had been brought up in the tradition that a rabbi's
family made sacrifices, he had grave apprehensions that his
wife and children might be wrenched too severely by their
coming exile. All the same, he looked forward to compensating advantages both for them and for himself. High on
the list was privacy. In tight-knit communities, even those
as large as the Jewish community of Portland, a man of the
cloth lives in a fishbowl. Every member of his family is
subjected to the steady gaze of the censorious and the curious. In New York, the precious, merciful gift of anonymity
can be had by stepping down into the subway or out into
the street. On the theory that rabbis and their families are
entitled to a reasonably normal existence, the Wises, in the
years that followed, reserved their intimate life for their
intimates. Jonah was concerned to keep intact the source at
which he renewed his strength; the thrusts and pressures of
the outside world were stopped at his front door.

Old friends were waiting in New York, ready to help
Jonah begin his new life. Adolph Ochs had been urging him
for years to come, and was now immensely pleased. An
enthusiastic letter of welcome full of wise advice came from
Dr. Leon Watters, who had known him in Cincinnati. Solomon Lowenstein and his wife made plans for a half-dozen
dinners and company evenings designed to introduce Jonah
and Helen Wise to all the bigwigs in Jewish affairs. Lowenstein was delighted with the prospect of reunion with an
old companion, especially an old companion who was so
valiant a *schnorrer* (as Jonah happily labeled himself in an
interview published in the Yiddish-language *Jewish Daily*

Forward in 1955; the word means "beggar") for important Jewish causes. Such *schnorrers* were invaluable to Lowenstein, who was a power in social work and director of the huge complex of the Federated Jewish Philanthropies. Ordained at Hebrew Union College in 1898, he had never served a congregation; the need for social services in a wildly proliferating urban society dictated a change in his vocation. He was a licensed clergyman, nevertheless, and frequently officiated at weddings and funerals. Lowenstein's expectation of superior aid in fund raising was to be fulfilled, but Jonah's expectation that Lowenstein would join Central Synagogue was not. Jonah was firmly wedded to the idea that every believer had a duty to affiliate with organized religion. Lowenstein stoutly refused to join any synagogue. He was a full-fledged rabbi, he said, ordained at HUC and licensed by the State of New York. Wherever he was there was also a congregation, for he conducted services privately. The divine worship at which he officiated was as acceptable to heaven as the Central Synagogue's. A paltry subterfuge, Jonah replied—not without some heat—and repudiation of Solomon's plain duty to set a responsible example. Jonah would not give up. Lowenstein would not give in. Between them, they kept the dispute alive until 1942, when Lowenstein died and a stricken Jonah conducted his funeral.

Jonah's last official act in Portland was to conduct a union Thanksgiving service with the Presbyterian church in which the burned-out Congregation Beth Israel had been given shelter. He and his family then took themselves to New York, where, on December 6, the congregation of Central Synagogue greeted its rabbi-elect at a testimonial dinner held at the Hotel Astor. On the evening of January

1, 1926, Stephen S. Wise once again installed Jonah, this time as the sixth rabbi of Central Synagogue.

The new home of the Jonah Wises was at 71 Central Park West, near 65th Street. Central Synagogue was a mile away, exactly the right distance to be traveled on foot in good weather. In his 34 years at Central, the longest incumbency in the congregation's long history, Jonah habitually walked to his office or to the synagogue. His most direct route to the synagogue ended in the heavily trafficked streets of central Manhattan, but its first two-thirds were passed in an Arcadian world of trees, grass, lakes, and bridle paths: the southern half of Central Park. In that peaceful daily expedition, he retrieved something of Portland's felicitous balance of natural and man-made landscape.

Central Synagogue was founded as Ahawath Chesed (Love of Mercy) congregation in 1846, the year in which Isaac Mayer Wise landed in New York. It is New York's third oldest Reform congregation; Rodeph Shalom and Emanu-El are older. (Central can be accounted the oldest if we date it from the founding of Shaar Hashomayim, which was merged with Ahawath Chesed at the turn of the century.) Its first rabbi, Dr. Adolph Huebsch, whom the congregation brought over from Bohemia in 1865, preached in German; and German did not fall into complete disuse until the onset of World War I. In 1870, Isaac Mayer Wise delivered the principal address at the laying of the cornerstone of the present building, which was designed by America's first Jewish architect, Henry Fernbach. It is the oldest synagogue house in continuous use in the city of New York. A landmark plaque erected by the New York Community Trust announces that "the style is Moorish Revival, the arrangement Gothic."

When Jonah B. Wise's ministry began, Central Synagogue was deeply imbedded in the previous century. The
old *Minhag America* was used instead of the *Union Prayer Book*
(although Isaac S. Moses, Rabbi Krass's predecessor, had
been a principal editor of the Union Prayer Book). Hats
were still worn by the president of the synagogue, the rabbi,
and other functionaries on the bema (the raised platform
before the sanctuary). The membership was narrowly
based. Dues-paying members were few for a house of worship so large, and all but a handful were from the older, or
"German" element in American Jewry. The program was
narrow. Religious education was offered in rented quarters
in two locations; although nearly 300 pupils attended, the
hours of instruction were minimal and the pay of teachers
extremely low. The rest of the program consisted of worship
on Friday evenings, Saturday mornings, festivals, and the
High Holy Days.

When Jonah's ministry ended, Central's big membership included all elements of American Jewry, "Russian" as
well as "German." Its program embraced a wide spectrum
of activities—social, cultural, religious—and appealed to
many interests on many levels. It reached into all parts of
the United States and Canada, and touched the lives of
gentiles as well as Jews.

Jonah's first act at Central was to exorcise one last
memory of the ghetto. He got the officers of the synagogue
to put aside their toppers. The maneuver by which he accomplished this objective was executed effortlessly and with
style. At the meeting called to plan his installation ceremony, he announced pleasantly to his somewhat startled trustees, "I am constitutionally unable to wear a hat in the
synagogue." After that, they could hardly wear hats,

either. The reform was overdue by the standards of progressive Judaism elsewhere. Some years later, however, this bit
of streamlining was to discourage the affiliation of a large
bloc of highly desirable prospective members who were
strongly attached to the ancient custom of covered heads at
prayer. There was a certain immediate loss, too. Rabbi
Krass, when minister of Central, had worn an absolutely
beautiful top hat. Albert Ottinger, a popular and respected
member of the board of trustees, had one that was no whit
inferior; he wore it a few times after Jonah's challenge and
then reluctantly put it back in its box. But Jonah might well
have said, with Michelangelo, "The more the marble
wastes, the more the statue grows."

Less impulse and more formal planning than this went
into the further transformation of Central. Mr. Hamburger
and the other trustees gave Jonah full co-operation and
support. The main concern of all was the younger generation. All institutions impelled to stay alive recognize that
they must address themselves to youth, for youth is, by
definition, the future. They do not always recognize as
well—Jonah did—that, in a rapidly changing world, the
older generation is, almost by definition, the past. If the
older generation tries to force its own feelings and patterns
of life upon the younger generation, its efforts are self-
defeating. In remaking Central, Jonah took his cues from
students and the young-married set. Their ideas about life
and religion were being absorbed from the larger society
that surrounded them, and were conspicuously different
from the ideas of their elders. Isaac Mayer Wise had
warned his coreligionists in 1854 that, unless the synagogue
meets the challenge and is harmonized with American
life, "we will have no Jews in this country in less than half

a century." In 1925 that thought was still to the point. And Jonah was determined that Central Synagogue, during his ministry, would not only be an expression of twentieth-century American life but a vital center of it.

Every time he talked to his rabbinical colleagues, his staff, the members of his congregation, the press, or the public, Jonah saw his philosophy of religion put to the stern test of its relevance to American life. His bent was not truly philosophical—he was too much a man of action for that—but he was consistent, clear, and earnest in what he believed. He matched action to idea with the sure touch of a master. A few paragraphs (here somewhat abridged) from a radio talk of the 1950s sum up views that guided him all his working life:

We Jews have been Americans from the earliest colonial life to this very day. We lived by and preserved the precious elements of American life long before Columbus. "America" is no longer a political term. "America" is the designation of an ideal. We are living in a great creative community. It has barely reached its first maturity. It is girding itself for newer and greater efforts toward the redemption of all mankind. We have taken part in two great international wars; in neither have we asked for conquered land, subjugated people, or enrichment through reparations. After this war, as after the last war, we generously supplied enormous amounts of relief in kind and in money for friend and enemy alike, steadily pursuing the cause of rescue and re-establishment of all human beings whom we can reach. This is Judaism as well as Americanism.

It seems to me that this determination to help comes directly from the Hebrew Scriptures. It carries into practice those admonitions which have for thousands of years guided and determined Jewish communal life. Certainly when one thinks of the greatest of all charity, the pity of one nation for another, one can easily realize the tremendous vigor and force of the Hebrew Scripture's ideal, which always presents itself with the idea "Have we not one Father? Has not one God created us? Why do we deal treacherously, every man against his brother?"

The world does not recognize nor does it understand the generous impulse of Americans to reach out a helping hand toward other nations of the world. Those other nations have not been nurtured, as America has been, on the sustaining milk of the Hebrew Scriptures. We Jews can rejoice in that blood kinship between our faith and the true faith of our beloved land.

We Americans are trying to achieve a great redemption. I want to preserve Judaism for Americans because it is the religion which frees my mind and liberates my soul. I want it to be preserved in every possible form so that I can pass it down to my children and my children's children. I want them to feel that it is their own, but not only for their own redemption. I want them to bring new powers, when new powers are wanted, to America, and through America to the world, as it was envisaged in the nineteenth chapter of *Leviticus*, where the Hebrew writer said, "Thou shalt love thy neighbor as thyself," as it was expressed by the prophet Amos when he said, "Justice runs down as water and righteousness as a mighty stream."

In all these things I see American Israel going toward a great redemption.

So wholehearted a ratification of Woodrow Wilson's claim that "America is the only idealistic nation on earth" came naturally to a man whose two fundamental allegiances did not come into conflict but actually reinforced each other.

The American national character, ever since visiting literary Europeans took note of its emergence, has been seen by the world as incorporating certain admirable but puzzling attitudes and judgments: sensitivity to oppression; a passion for justice; a haunted sense of responsibility for the actions and the well-being of the community; a belief in religion as right conduct rather than ritual or creed; commitment to human brotherhood; and above all, perhaps, a vision of a coming just and peaceful world— to be achieved, of course, through the universal adoption of the American way of life. Such qualities of mind are not really puzzling to persons who have leafed through the pages of *Jeremiah*, *Amos*, *Micah*, and the *Psalms*. Small wonder that Will Herberg could observe that, "by being Jewish," the immigrant Jews "were, in a very curious way, becoming more typically American….the most 'American' of all the ethnic groups that went into the making of modern America."

The scale of values that the world recognizes as distinctively American, and stamped indelibly on the American national character by the founding fathers of New England, was indeed shaped by the Bible. The Pilgrims left the Old World to enter "the New Israel." Cotton Mather, in paying tribute to the memory of John Winthrop, used these words:

When the Noble Design of carrying a Colony of Chosen People into an American Wilderness, was by some Eminent Persons undertaken, This Eminent Person was, by the Consent of all, Chosen for the Moses.

The following words preface the law code of Plymouth Colony:

It was the great privilege of Israel of Old and so was acknowledged by them, Nehemiah the 9th and 10th, that God gave them right Judgments and true Lawes. They are for the mayne so exemplary, being grounded on principles of moral equity... that we have had an eye principally unto the aforesaid platforme in the framing of this small body of Lawes.

America ceased to be a theocratic community long ago, and the puritan conscience has revolved into the secular sphere; but the origins of American social ideals could not be plainer. The puritan fathers had the Law and the prophets in their bones.

Jonah's perception that Jews as Jews and Americans as Americans endorsed a surprisingly congruent set of historic values affected his entire commerce with his environment. It led to his absorption with Abraham Lincoln's life and writings, to his earnest promotion of interfaith understanding, even to his pleasure in camaraderie with the Christian ministry. And it led to unprecedented strength for Central Synagogue, which, on his accession to its pulpit, entered a period of orderly and sustained growth.

Jonah had an agenda for the business of consolidating and expanding Central Synagogue, and on it community activities had the highest priority. He saw a rich community program as the necessary mortar of a solid organizational structure for the synagogue. As a young rabbi in Portland, he had pioneered in expanding the community role of Beth Israel, discovering without surprise that strong religious schools, boys' clubs, gatherings, and opportunities for creative synagogal work were far more effective than unsupplemented prayers and sermons in bringing synagogues and the people close together. A city championship won by the basketball team of the Temple Beth Israel boys' club had half-won the cause of religion among his teenagers.

Even athletics, then, could be a tool in the service of religion! And, if basketball accomplished much for the children of the privileged, it accomplished wonders for the children of the poor. It helped the children of the immigrants on Portland's West Side to rally from the rude shocks of poverty, dislocation, and depressing surroundings. Equally important, it introduced them to a kind of experience that they desperately needed. The Jews of Eastern Europe were lamentably insensitive to a large part of life. To cultivate physical vitality, strength, and grace was something that never even entered their heads. They did not engage in demanding physical sport. Their physical modesty was inordinate. The saying of Walt Whitman, a poet much loved by Jonah and a constant source of inspiration to him, that "the body is not more than the soul" and the soul "not more than the body" might have confirmed some of their notions about gentiles, but in all other ways it would have been found absurd. They knew beyond the reach of argument that the body was gross, not to be trusted, and rather un-Jewish. The young girl Tzeitl, in the song "Matchmaker, Matchmaker," does not ask for a bridegroom tanned and well-knit. She wants one "slender and pale." The Anatevkas of *Fiddler on the Roof* have vanished into memory, and nowhere but in a few dwindling enclaves of medievalism are the Jews still on the outs with their corporeal selves.

No space for community activity was available to the congregation on the day that Jonah was installed; not even the most modest program was possible. Money had been raised for a community house, however, and the board had been negotiating with the YWCA over purchase of a fairly commodious old building at 35 East 62nd Street, eight blocks from the synagogue house. Within the month, negotiations were concluded and a purchase contract signed. The community program could now be launched. The building on 62nd Street served the congregation well until 1965, when it was sold and construction began on the

new $2,500,000 Jonah B. Wise Community Center across
the street from the synagogue house.

Jonah lost little time in getting started. He set up his
study on the top floor of the new community house in two
sunny rooms. Two rooms were required for his rather extensive library, which included many treasures brought to
the New World by Jonas Bondi in 1859; these Jonah regarded as being held in trust for Hebrew Union College, to
which they were eventually left. At the same time, he began
to ready the building to receive the religious school, whose
two centers were now to be consolidated.

The religious school was put on a firmer basis, with a
stronger curriculum and professional standards of education. Its pupils were accorded an active part in the educational process: they conducted their own affairs and put out
their own mimeographed publication. One room in the
community house was set aside for a school library, which
was equipped with open shelves, reading tables, and comfortable chairs. The library was later named for Max
Schallek, who succeeded Mr. Hamburger as president of
the synagogue. The religious school joined the religious
schools of other Reform congregations to form a city-wide
organization. In 1927, Jonah organized and led a huge
rally of religious school pupils at the Century Theater.
Three thousand children attended.

Before long, Central was armed with—for the times—a
full panoply of auxiliary organizations. A fair-sized little
republic had come into being, with Jonah in charge as its
chief executive. All age groups and interests were represented, and even the smallest citizen participated in its
work. All the constituent groups provided social fellowship,
education, and cultural enrichment. The Youth Group and

Junior Congregation, for instance, published their own newspapers and staged intramural debates and theatrical productions. These two groups were incubators for subsequent activists and leaders. J. Jacques Stone, vice-president of Central Synagogue and, at this writing, director of adult education in New York for the Temple Brotherhoods, was head of the Junior Congregation in the 1930s. The two major auxiliary organizations were the Brotherhood and the Sisterhood, the men's group and the women's. Their work was carried on simultaneously on four different levels: for the synagogue directly; for the Jewish community; for the larger community of metropolitan New York; and for the nation. A good deal of it was planned and executed on an interchurch-interfaith basis in concert with like institutions. The Brotherhood offered an extensive adult education program of forums and lectures to the members of Central Synagogue, and sponsored one of the strongest Boy Scout programs anywhere. Steady support was given the Jewish Chautauqua Society, the educational arm of the National Federation of Temple Brotherhoods. The Lexington School for the Deaf, an agency of the Federation of Jewish Charities of New York, was the object of special attention. Aid to this institution included religious services in sign language held annually at Central on festivals and the High Holy Days. The Brotherhood also held an annual service for the Jewish staff members of the New York office of the United States Customs Service. The needs of the larger community of city and state were not forgotten, especially on emergency occasions, when the Brotherhood joined social and governmental agencies in special drives and projects. The Sisterhood took charge of the synagogue's receptions and other hospitality functions. In addition, its sewing project produced a sizable volume of clothing, which was distributed to needy children in the public schools by the New York City Board of Education. Use of the synagogue vestry was extended to the Jewish Child Care Association of New York for receptions for foster parents, and to the New York Council of the Girl Scouts for craft exhibitions. The Federation of Jewish Charities was given major assistance with its camping programs for underprivileged children and with the work of its dozen-or-so hospitals and medical-care centers. In its work for the larger community, the Sisterhood took aid to the blind as its special province. Work in this area cut across all sectarian lines: the Sisterhood was an integral part of the interchurch-interfaith group that supplied "talking books" and "sight-savers" (i.e., reading matter printed in jumbo-size type legible to persons with as little as 10 per cent vision) both locally and nationally. The Senior League and the Young Married Group, Central's two other auxiliary organizations, also performed important civic functions, although on a smaller scale. They had a rich social and cultural program.

Jonah personally rounded out the educational and cultural offerings of Central's family of organizations with Sunday-morning "conferences," which consisted of lectures, readings, and music. After his first years, Central had the connections and the talent to present first-class concert performances of Jewish sacred music, and used those resources to make a unique contribution to New York's musical life. At Beth Israel, as early as 1919, Jonah had instituted the public display of Jewish liturgical art, mainly textiles and silver. Cups for the *Kiddush* (the ceremony of the sanctification of the wine), seven- and eight-branched candlesticks, and such paraphernalia belonging to the

Scrolls of the Law as *yods* (pointers ending in a fist with extended index finger), embroidered covers, and silver breastplates and crowns, had been arrayed in glass-topped cases. He installed a similar display in the public lobby of Central's community house. It was also possible, in a city like New York, to hold art exhibitions of a more general nature. The first of these was in 1928. Central's outstanding exhibition was a one-man show in 1952 of work by a member, James N. Rosenberg. A leading member of the American bar and a dedicated, tireless worker for international relief and reconstruction and for international peace through law, Rosenberg was one of several important Jewish figures who joined Central because of their working association with Jonah. He began to paint after he retired from his law practice, and soon revealed an unexpected talent for imaginative landscape, a talent that led to the acquisition of his paintings by a number of the country's foremost art museums. Rosenberg donated one landscape from his big show to the synagogue. It hung for many years in the conference room of the community house, and will occupy a place of central importance in the new Jonah B. Wise Community Center.

The proliferation of the nondevotional functions of the church and the synagogue—for Central's expansion was typical, not unusual—has been seen by some observers as contrary to the true spirit of religion. The most significant experience that religion holds out to humanity, they tell us —the sense of a divine presence—is made to fade into the background. Jonah, needless to say, was no subscriber to this view. He did not believe that inner spirituality suffered when the churches broadened their function, no matter how much or how little religious attitudes were in evidence. The relief of man's estate was work that he considered holy.

Jonah also saw spiritual value at its highest in the interfaith movement of the period between two wars. The 1920s were disfigured by the rebirth of the Ku Klux Klan, the 1930s by the ascendancy of fascism in Europe and the spread of fascist influence in the United States. These developments jolted the American religious community into mounting a vigorous counteroffensive. Inasmuch as tribal insularity was clearly the fuel on which the flames of hatred and aggression fed, the response was, of necessity, organized on an interfaith basis. The movement affirmed the basic unity of the great variety of population elements in American society. Catholic-Protestant-Jewish co-operation in civic work and public information became a normal feature of American life, and there was a vast increase in Protestant-Jewish pulpit exchange and joint worship. Jonah's participation in the interfaith movement was energetic and wholehearted, as it had been in interfaith activity from his first days in the ministry. In the past thirty years, the interfaith aspect of civic and religious life in America has become steadily more prominent. At the same time, prejudice, it would appear, has been fighting a desperate rear-guard action against increasingly heavy odds. For this encouraging development, the present generation of Americans owes some measure of gratitude to Jonah and his colleagues of many denominations a generation ago.

Jonah must have taken a good deal of satisfaction in the sturdy growth of interfaith. His father had been an early pioneer, having exchanged pulpits and participated in union Thanksgiving services around the time of the Civil War. In addition, participation in interfaith activity enriched Jonah's own life with many pleasant associations and two devoted friends, the Rev. Dr. Ralph W. Sockman, pastor of Christ Church Methodist, and the Rev. Dr. Theodore C. Speers, pastor of Central Presbyterian Church. Both churches were on Park Avenue in the low sixties, just a few blocks north of Central Synagogue and, therefore, ideal institutional partners for pulpit exchanges, union services, and co-operative lecture series. The three men found a good deal more than compatibility in their interrelationship. They were all thoroughly similar in background, point of view, and even sense of humor—always ready and a little sharp. They took delight in one another's company and sustenance from their friendship in times of stress. Such times came, for Sockman and Speers each lost a young and beloved son and Jonah his wife. In 1966, Christ Church, Central Presbyterian, and Central Synagogue will celebrate their thirtieth union Thanksgiving service. The first such service was held some months after Ted Speers arrived in New York and Jonah was the first minister of any faith to reach out to him with an invitation—on that occasion to lunch with Mary Woolley, president of Mount Holyoke and a leading activist in the cause of world peace, and Stanley King, president of Amherst. In 1947, Jonah had the pleasure, at a ceremony honoring Speers' father, Robert Elliot Speers, the retired secretary of the Presbyterian Board of Foreign Missions, of making the presentation: a bible that had once belonged to George Washington.

The New York circles in which Jonah moved were more tightly drawn than those he had frequented on the West Coast. In Portland, his grass-roots connections had been many, and his concern for workingmen, rebels, and dissenters had brought him offbeat friends. In New York, his working contacts were increasingly high-level. He found himself most often in the company of the well-placed and well-off.

This change of social climate was not inconsequential. For one thing, his friendships no longer provided him with the entertainment of intellectual play. His formidable intelligence needed something to feed upon; and it fed upon work, upon management, on administration, on the framing of policies and decisions. He could hardly get enough of this kind of mental exercise.

Personal friendship became a kind of extracurricular pleasure in which he forgot that he was a rabbi or a top executive of the JDC, a man whose wrong decision could bring disaster to a multitude. At the Metropolis Country Club, in White Plains, which he joined not long after moving to the East Coast, he could be just a man among men. To carry around a few well-used golf clubs in a shabby old bag rather than an expensively cased and impressively gleaming arsenal was a form of personal indulgence.

Metropolis had originally been named "Freundschaft" —"friendship"—and rather appropriately, too. Its atmosphere was informal and its membership companionable. Jonah's particular friends at Metropolis were Billy Nathan, a physician; Ed Waterman, "the Czar"; Milton Greenebaum; Jesse Jelenko; and Ben Theise. He was perfectly natural with these gentlemen and disported himself like a boy.

The man through whom Jonah became a Metropolis member was Ben Theise, the youngest of the little group and golf champion of the club in the later 1920s. He was the nephew of Portland's Ben Selling, after whom he was named. At Selling's behest, Jonah had looked him up after coming East. Metropolis, thus, was a link with Portland's

Tualatin Country Club. As in Portland, Jonah's unquench-
able enthusiasm for gardening in all its forms landed him
the office of greens-committee chairman. The finest greens
in Westchester County became his goal, and, with his
customary thoroughness, he equipped himself by spending
a term of study at Columbia.

Jonah was asked to officiate at the funeral of Theise's
mother, a Christian Scientist. He did so willingly, and, out
of respect to the deceased and to a sister religion, performed
the ceremony in a genuinely Christian Science manner, as
Mrs. Theise would have wished.

When the opportunity presented itself, he renewed his
contact with labor and his old friends the immigrant Jews
of Orthodox extraction. On the second day of every festival
—just another day to the Reformed—he invariably showed
up at an Orthodox or Conservative synagogue. When he
was sought out in 1935 by a group of garment workers to
take on a rather burdensome assignment, he accepted,
although he was up to his ears in work and responsibility
and no one could have blamed him if he had said no. He
became treasurer and representative of the Workers Aim
Association, through which the group dealt with the Farm
Resettlement Administration. That New Deal agency had
allocated $500,000—a large sum in those days—to buy
1200 acres near Hightstown, New Jersey, where it proposed
to resettle two hundred garment workers and their families.
The project was given the name of Jersey Homesteads, and
was to be a co-operative of two hundred homes, a factory,
and a truck, dairy, and poultry farm. Jonah found himself
holding a $31,000 fund placed in his care by 62 members of
the Workers Aim. Each was to put up an initial $500 for a
house and two acres of land. The project became operative

in the summer of 1936, when fifty families moved in. Jonah's responsibilities ceased in 1940, when government participation in Hightstown was liquidated, and the members of the co-operative became full-fledged individual homeowners.

His liberal convictions never changed, nor did his general social outlook. He continued to feel that radicals prodded sleeping consciences and drew guidelines for constructive social change. He insisted on their right to be heard. He was an Al Smith supporter in the 1928 Presidential election. His commitment to the New Deal and FDR was early and wholehearted; and he wept in the pulpit on the April day that he held a memorial service for the wartime President.

Jonah's life underwent a dramatic change in the 1930s, when events propelled him into a position of national prominence. The disastrous spiral of world depression and political upheaval shook the foundations of Jewish existence in Europe, and the men who led the key organizations of American Jewry called him to a high place in their councils. Over a thirty-year span, the claims upon his strength were enormous. He could have taken an extended leave of absence from congregational work or relinquished it altogether in order to handle his new responsibilities unhindered. Some of his newer associates urged this step upon him, but he resisted their promptings. He cherished his calling of rabbi and his association with Central, which was all that he could have wished it to be. He was also willing to assume an appalling burden of work—a matter both of personal pride and of sublime self-confidence in his ability to do just about anything. Such a picture of his own powers turned out to be astonishingly close to the truth. His apt and splendidly conditioned body was equal to the most exacting demands of work and travel. Of necessity, however, a considerable share of his pulpit and congregational duties fell to his assistant rabbi, Saul Applebaum, and he himself became far less accessible to his congregation and the public, for he had to husband his energy and forestall invasions upon his time.

The story of his massive efforts on the national and world scale is told in Chapter 6, "The Message of Israel," which deals with his pioneering radiocasts, and Chapter 7, "The JDC and the UJA," which deals with his role in international rescue and relief. Chapter 5 continues with the story of his professional life and civic activities during his middle years.

Secondarily, the disaster in Europe was of benefit to other continents. The many artists, scientists, and scholars of the first rank who left the Old World for the New have contributed greatly to the present flourishing condition of learning and the arts in America. ("Hitler has been a good friend to me," Walter Cook, the late chairman of New York University's Department of Fine Arts used to say happily when he talked about a stellar group of refugee scholars who turned his department into the most dazzling institute of its kind anywhere. "He shook the tree, and I picked up the apples.") Jonah and the Central Synagogue were early beneficiaries. A member of the synagogue, Mrs. Hubert Mann, was chairman of the Council of Jewish Women's Committee on Artists in 1937. "Would you be interested in singing on a religious program, *The Message of Israel*?" she asked Frederick Lechner, a baritone whom the Council had helped bring over the year before. "Rabbi Jonah Wise wants to raise its standards." Lechner was interested. A meeting was arranged, and he came around to see Jonah.

The two men hit it off right away. Jonah opened the interview with his usual test procedure: he dropped a remark calculated to throw his vis-à-vis off balance and then sat back to observe the reaction. His compatriots, as a rule, could play this game with him fairly well, and so could Englishmen. Frenchmen were better at it than anybody, but most Germans were completely floored. With Lechner, his gambit was to ask, "Are you married?" and when the other man answered, "Yes," to say musingly, "My, my. Whoever told you to do such a foolish thing?" Lechner merely blinked. But when the conversation got around to music and Jonah propounded (quite seriously) a well-worn theory of his that "the best church music is third rate," the singer said to the rabbi, "Nothing is too good for the Lord."

Jonah was tickled by the reply. He was a little formidable, he knew; and many persons whom he dealt with truckled to him. But he passionately wanted them not to. Clearly, this Lechner was a likable fellow.

Lechner was made musical director and first soloist of *The Message of Israel.* As musical director, he replaced Isidore Weinstock, who was then the cantor of Central Synagogue; Weinstock was not well, and needed to restrict his activities. Jonah wanted Lechner to have a free hand in rebuilding the program's musical identity, which was intended thenceforward to breathe as modern and universal a spirit in its musical as in its verbal offerings. At once, he dismissed the organist and choir.

"What are you doing?" Lechner said to him. "They're very good." The group was rehired without delay.

Jonah's reservations about his singers had nothing to do with their competence, although he was not completely

aware of that. He was not unmusical by popular standards
—that is, he listened to music and went to musical events,
sometimes enjoying the experience. But he was most unmusical by Lechner's standards, which were sky-high.
Jonah's real quarrel was with the music that the group performed. It was the traditional synagogue music that he had
characterized years before in Portland as "too archaic and
too narrowly associated with one tone and one thought...a
memory...a dirge of ghettos, Wailing Walls, and wildernesses...." Even so, he had no wish to eliminate the traditional music from his order of worship altogether; he wanted
to leave enough for seasoning, enough to preserve an essential link with the ancestral past. But he did want the sacred
music of the synagogue and everything else that had to do
with the practice of Judaism to be part of an open world,
not a world that closed in upon itself.

To Weinstock, the traditional music of the synagogue
was the only music for the synagogue. He saw no reason to
indulge the whims of a rabbi he had known as a small child
(he had been Isaac Mayer Wise's cantor in Cincinnati in
earlier years) and felt that the senior Wise had put the
capstone on the whole structure of Reform Judaism. Isaac
Mayer Wise himself had not felt that way at all; for instance, he cheerfully accepted the *Union Prayer Book* as a
step forward from his own *Minhag America*. Nevertheless,
the shape of worship in Plum Street Temple was as tied
to its antecedents as the first gasoline buggy to the horse-
drawn carriage—whipsocket and all. (Such is the anato-
my of change.) Isaac Mayer Wise's graceful bow to the
Union Prayer Book occurred in 1894; in 1926, when Jonah
arrived, Weinstock was still holding out against its adoption at Central Synagogue. It took Jonah no less than two

years to force the changeover from the *Minhag America*.

Four weeks after Lechner went to work for Jonah, Weinstock died. Central Synagogue was without a cantor.

The cantor is the central figue in the public worship of the Jews. He stands at its liturgical and architectural focus, the altar, while his sung verse and the congregation's massed response build a symmetrical edifice of sound. A cantor is more needed than a rabbi. Rabbis are neither celebrants nor priests; they are teachers. Liturgically speaking, they play no part at all—or played no part before the disappearance of a laity steeped in synagogal ways forced an active role upon them.

It was important, then, for Central to find a new cantor at the earliest possible moment. A committee was appointed to interview applicants, of whom there were many, and select Weinstock's successor.

Jonah had an idea in his head. Perhaps the best road to his wished-for musical reform was no cantor at all. But could the sacred service, that complex, historically evolved art form, sustain its power without the cantor's visible presence? Perhaps.

"Lechner," he said. "Will you meet with the committee and agree to sing the cantor's part from the choir loft until we come to a decision?" A first-class soloist in the choir loft might well be the answer to his problem. Lechner a-greed.

The committee members were relieved to have Lechner stand by. The less pressure upon them to make a quick decision, the less likelihood of a selection that they might later regret. And, musically, the cantorless service turned out to be irreproachable. Devotionally, however, it was less successful; its elements did not fuse into a heightened unity. The trustees wanted to have a cantor at the altar.

"All right," Jonah said to them. "If you must have a cantor, then I want Lechner." He was not to be diverted from his musical reform.

Lechner had never thought of becoming a cantor. But he thought about it then, for Jonah's desire for a broader repertory and higher performance level in synagogue music had struck a responsive chord. He wanted to go on with what the two of them had started.

"If I say yes," he said finally, "I must have complete freedom to continue with my concert and operatic singing."

"All the better!" Jonah answered gaily. "It will reflect credit on the synagogue."

Lechner's colleagues in the world of music tore their hair. His career, they said, had been destroyed. Lechner went on to a thoroughly satisfactory career in the concert hall, the opera house, the broadcasting studio, and the synagogue. From 1943 to 1950 he was a baritone in the Metropolitan Opera Company, and received particularly favorable notices for his performances in Wagner's *Nibelungen Ring* and Strauss's *Rosenkavalier*. He has been cantor of Central Synagogue ever since his appointment in May 1938. No other cantor in history has been heard by so many people.

With its rabbi and cantor both working hard at the project, Central Synagogue became invested with the rich, poetic order of worship for which it has been celebrated for decades.

Jonah and Lechner worked well together, shared common goals, and were in basic agreement about most things. But it must not be imagined that between two such men unruffled harmony could prevail a hundred per cent of the

time. Both were full of ideas, which they discussed constantly, argued about often, and fought over occasionally. For
Jonah music was a means to an end, for Lechner an end in
itself; this was the source of their occasional clashes, invariably over the *Message of Israel*. Like all other producers—
religious or secular—who aim for a saturation audience,
Jonah was concerned to keep his program genuinely popular in its appeal. He was not in the least averse to homely
touches, such as common hymns or choral offerings by the
children of the synagogue. "If you are going to stoop so low
as to schedule that moronic hymn you want me to sing,"
Lechner would say between his teeth after subjection to
heavy pressure, "I'll sing it, but you'll have to get right
down there with me and cheapen your sermon, too."
Jonah also could generate considerable warmth in debate;
and sometimes apologies were in order from one or the
other. They were always made. Jonah could not imagine
how he had ever got along without his younger colleague.
Lechner was deeply thankful for the stability brought into
a life so thoroughly disrupted by events in Germany, and
for the assistance he had received in bringing his brother to
the United States. And the two men had genuine affection
for each other as well as ties of obligation and respect;
their quarrels were family quarrels.

Lechner was given ministerial status, and performed
weddings and funerals. He often went along when Jonah
accepted an out-of-town invitation as guest rabbi. The
first such expedition was to Cornell, where they were
jointly to conduct a service and Jonah was to preach a
sermon. On the train, Jonah said, "Don't be surprised if I
don't want to have breakfast with you. I'm always alone at
breakfast. I'm a beast in the morning. I'm like that at home,

too." Years of heavy travel had taught him that when he was on the road he needed an hour or two of solitude every day in order to avoid being hammered into exhaustion. Lechner heeded the warning and ate breakfast by himself. A student, the son of a member of Central, had not been warned. He saw Jonah in the dining room and wanted to sit at his table. To his discomfiture and surprise, Jonah would not let him.

Shortly after the United States entered World War II, Lechner got word that his parents were victims of Hitler's "final solution." He was overcome by the news, and although able to perform his duties, went about in blackest misery. He said nothing about his loss to anyone except his wife; he could not talk about it. Jonah tried to find out why his friend was so depressed.

"Are you in financial need?" he asked.

"No," Lechner replied. Finally, he told Jonah what was wrong.

Jonah was silent for a moment before speaking again.

"I'll tell you what I want you to do. I am doing this for my own sake, because I need you. I know how much you like the country. Go there. Put on an old pair of pants. Take as much time as you want. Stay in the country until you've recovered. Then come back, because we have to have you here."

He gave the younger man enough of a lift so that he was able to overcome his depression.

During the years that followed, Lechner, ably assisted by Lazar Weiner, choirmaster, and Alexander Richardson, organist, provided the congregation of Central Synagogue with memorable music. On New Year's Day and the Day of Atonement he gave them melodies from their childhood.

Once a year, he presented a special musical service with organ, choir, and himself as soloist. Jonah let him do anything he wished for this annual feature, and backed him with extensive publicity and advertising. Concerts included Bloch's *Sacred Service*; Charlotte Garden's *Song of Amos*; *Music of the Synagogue from Antiquity to the Present Time*—for this program Lechner revived works by L'Ebreo ("the Jew," in Italian), who was Salomone Rossi of Mantua, an exact contemporary of Monteverdi in neighboring Venice and a leading seventeenth-century Italian composer; and a liturgical-music festival of contemporary composers. The program creating the biggest stir was Darius Milhaud's *Sacred Service*, given twice in live performance, and, through records and broadcasts, heard all over the world.

Lechner was not the only exile from Germany helped by Jonah and Central toward re-establishment in the New World. The synagogue house and community center were thrown open to a large group of German Jews, numbering close to a thousand families. Their spiritual leader was Rabbi Hugo Hahn, a man of great dignity and reserve, scholarly in habit and immersed in Old World ways.

Hahn came to America in 1939 after his home and his synagogue in Essen had been burned down by SS men. His cousin, Mrs. Bessie Campe, who was connected with the refugee service in New York, brought him to Jonah's attention and asked whether something might not be done to help him resume his interrupted career.

"I can give shelter to his organization," said Jonah, "and have him serve his people as my assistant rabbi, but I cannot pay him."

The German rabbi was well pleased with this arrangement, and, for the next four years, used the synagogue vestry for religious services and the community house for lectures and meetings. He was warmed by the fraternal consideration shown him by his host, and was supremely grateful for assistance without which the congregation that he now heads might never have been formed. He admired Jonah's courage, energy, and wholehearted devotion to the cause of rescuing the Jews of Europe. But American Reform Judaism, which Jonah exemplified in concentrated form, was a bit of a shock to him. Jonah's first words to Hahn were, "Whether I'm a good Jew I'm not quite sure. But I am sure I'm a good American."

One day soon after, he asked Hahn, "How long have you been in America?"

"Three months."

"And you have been in New York all that time. You must know that New York is not really America. That's one of our sayings. I will show you America. I have to make a money-raising tour for the UJA. Come with me; I'll pay your way. And I'll see to it that I get my money's worth."

They went to Detroit, Pittsburgh, Cincinnati, and Chicago. America was shown to Hahn; Hahn, "a man from the land of Hitler," was shown to America. Pledges to the UJA went up and up.

In Pittsburgh, Jonah took Hahn along with him to radio station WPIT, where he wanted to see the program director about a better time for *The Message of Israel*. He had to wait. A monument of patience in many ways, he could not bear to be kept sitting and sitting in an outer office. When he could stand it no longer, he sent in a message: "I can't wait any more. If you can't see me now, I'll have to leave." The man saw him. Trying to get things straight, he said:

"You are Stephen Wise." There it was again!

"No, I'm not Stephen! I'm Jonah! Jonah B. Wise, the *Message of Israel* man." But he got the time that he wanted and left the office in a happy frame of mind.

They were in Detroit over the weekend.

"Jonah," he was asked, "will you come out to the country club and play golf with us this Sunday?"

"Yes," he replied. "But the people I play with will have to contribute $500 apiece to the UJA." That work had to go on even in Jonah's moments of relaxation!

And when, after four years under Central's wing, Hahn was preparing to move his flock to new quarters and a separate existence, Jonah took him aside for a quick briefing on how, in a dynamic and abundant economy, infant organizations are systematically brought to maturity in the shortest possible time. The advice given was practical and forthright, the embodiment of American confidence in a secure future. There was genuine economic sophistication in it, not unrelated to the Keynesian "welfare economics" which would later escort the world to a new level of prosperity and to which young economists were then beginning to give detailed expression.

"The first thing that you and your congregation must acquire is a deficit," Jonah said. "Not a great big one, necessarily, but big enough to let you know it's there. It will spur you on to your best efforts and help you to create the kind of vigorous, hard-working organization you're going to need in order to deal with it effectively."

Thirty years ago, such a philosophy was rank heresy in countries like Germany and Switzerland. Even today in those lands, where the installment system is novel and daring, the purchase of things as necessary, durable, and expensive as houses, home furnishings, and cars is almost unthinkable before a man has cash in hand. Hahn could hardly believe his ears, and could only hope that Jonah was joking. Jonah may have expressed himself a little quizzically—as we have seen, it was in his nature to do so—but he was not joking at all.

At one time, Jonah may have entertained the hope that Hahn and his German Jews would become a permanent part of Central Synagogue. But the gaps in ideas and practices were too great to be bridged easily. The Germans could not be expected to think of Judaism and Americanism as basic identities—at least, not then. Judaism Jonah-style was not quite the historic Judaism to which they were accustomed. They themselves, adherents of liberal Judaism though they were, above all were wearers of hats! Accordingly, they established themselves as an independent religious organization, Congregation Habonim, with temporary headquarters at the United Order of True Sisters building on West 85th Street. Thereafter, they built their own synagogue house on West 66th Street, with a branch in Elmhurst and a youth center in Rego Park. (Presumably, they managed to do all this without incurring a deficit.) At this writing, they are a very solid part of the religious scene in New York. Fraternal ties bind them to Central Synagogue, and Central's members take deep satisfaction in having had a co-operative share in Habonim's rather considerable accomplishment.

✡ VI ✡

The Message of Israel

EVERY SEVEN DAYS, from 200 radio stations of the American Broadcasting Company and additional stations of the Armed Forces Radio Service, the *Message of Israel* is heard by millions of listeners on six continents. It opens with the intonation of the "Shema," the affirmation of the oneness of God. The "Shema" is followed by an anthem in which a round and flowing baritone voice mingles with organ strains and the blended voices of a massed choir. The program moderator discusses the choice of music, and elucidates its significance. Then, for a quarter-hour, comes a sermon, a lecture, or an interview. Another musical selection completes the radio service; the local station identifies itself against a background melody played softly on the organ; and the program goes off the air. A religious service has reached a vast number of nonchurchgoers in their own homes. And servicemen far from their families, dwellers on remote farms, ailing and infirm persons cut off from the outside world, and lonely people every-

where have had the healing of spiritual companionship.
Only half an hour has passed, but it has been so musicianly,
so carefully shaped, so artfully timed, that listeners have
been left with a sense of completeness.

Jonah Wise created the *Message of Israel,* and ran it for
25 years. During that time, the program originated from
the sanctuary of his own Central Synagogue. It does so
still. Except for technicians supplied by the network—
originally NBC's Blue Network, which became ABC in the
1940s when NBC was ordered by the courts to divest itself
of one of its two systems—the permanent staff of the
program came from the Central Synagogue ministry:
soloist, choirmaster, choir, organist, rabbi. Occasional help
was received from the staff of the Union of American
Hebrew Congregations and its president, Dr. Maurice N.
Eisendrath.

"I have had the privilege of cooperating with him,"
said David Sarnoff of Jonah in 1951, "in the development
of religious broadcasting....Nearly twenty years ago, as a
teacher wishing to transmit knowledge to the greatest
possible audience, he founded the *Message of Israel* program,
which he has been guiding ever since. In addition, he has
served as Jewish consultant to the Church of the Air since
its inception and participated in the organization of the
Eternal Light series, which is now being heard each week by
more than six million Americans. Jonah Wise, who saw in
radio a superb instrument for mass education, has been a
pioneer in Jewish religious broadcasting. I speak from
intimate knowledge when I tell you that he is one of those
men who are primarily responsible for the important place
which the national networks have given to the transmission
of religious values."

It was no accident that the foundation of the *Message* accompanied three important historic developments: the growth of unrestrained antisemitism, the establishment of the New Deal, and radio's coming of age.

In 1933 the rising forces of militant antidemocracy took the offensive in a world war of ideas. American echoes of German National Socialism reverberated along the air waves, turning the impact of radio to sinister uses. Perhaps the most conspicuous among those echoes was Father Coughlin's *Social Justice*, an organization and a publication as well as a national radio program. Father Coughlin laid the plight of the unemployed and the miseries of the world to the evil-doings of capitalistic international bankers and godless communistic agitators—the Jews, of course, constituting both varieties of malefactor. But radio also spoke for the democratic ideal, and in a strong, clear voice.

By 1930, radio receiving sets had been freed of the mess and clutter of headphones, speaker assemblies, wet batteries, chargers, regiments of knobs and dials, and hopeless tangles of multicolored wire. They were unitary, tidy, practical, and cheap. Anybody could now work a radio receiver; every family had room for one; and, depression or no, every family had one. Commercial broadcasting was big business. The major networks had emerged. The singing commercial had been invented. The whole radio enterprise (like television today) was dominated by advertising and beamed at the biggest possible mass audience. Although hardly geared to a gourmet level of taste, stations and networks had a commitment (in accordance with obligations imposed by the licensing provisions of the FCC) to "public service." They were as yet unarmed with the sure knowledge that they could safely ignore outcries that they spoon-fed the public a stupefying diet of imbecility, violence, and crime; and the full lethal force of popularity rating upon programing had not yet been unleashed. Accordingly, the networks made room for religious and cultural broadcasting. And they opened doors (not too many, not too wide) for experimentation with new forms and expressive techniques appropriate to the radio medium. Arranging words and sounds in bold new patterns, Archibald MacLeish, Norman Corwin, Orson Welles, Millard Lampell, Earl Robinson, and John Latouche founded a new radio literature—terse, rhythmic, vivid, contemporary in spirit, and as actual as a newspaper.

The new radio, in a sense, was the child of the New Deal. The Federal Arts Project of the WPA gave material assistance to talent of all kinds. Young talent had a flowering in which radio shared. Its creative writers caught the excitement of an era in which faith in the democratic tradition—blurred by postwar disillusionment and shaken by the spectacle of a helpless government and a stagnant nation—achieved a triumphant rebirth.

Radio, thus, was a proved and tested weapon of persuasion, reaching into every home and equipped with a growing literary tradition of its own, when, in the early 1930s, it became necessary for the Jews of America to come to their own defense against rampant antisemitism of a particularly virulent form. National radio had been available to them for many years, as a matter of fact, and available free, but no responsible Jewish group had created an instrument to take advantage of the opportunity. The National Broadcasting Company, upon its foundation in 1926, set up a citizen's council to advise it on the public interest. The advisory council's committee on religious activities, the Rev. Charles Macfarland, the Hon. Morgan J. O'Brien, and Julius Rosenwald, submitted guidelines for NBC's service to the three major American religions. The committee's recommendations provided for the widest possible broadcast of religious messages, nonsectarian in appearl and conducted by outstanding leaders of the several faiths. NBC accepted the committee's recommendations and opened conversations with Catholic, Protestant, and Jewish groups looking to the formation of suitable radio committees for sponsorship of religious programs. The National Council of Churches of Christ immediately organized its National Religious Radio Committee, whose *National Radio Pulpit*, in 1928, continued on a network basis the broadcasts begun five years before on WEAF, New York, by Dr. S. Parkes Cadman of Brooklyn. In 1930 the *Catholic Hour* began regular weekly broadcasts under the auspices of the National Council of Catholic Men. A Jewish program took on actuality when Felix Warburg, in 1934, formed the United Jewish Layman's Committee and became its first chairman. The other Layman's Committee members included Harold Hirsch, Edmund J. Kaufman, Albert D. Lasker, Fred Lazarus, Leo Lehman, and Henry Weinman. All were men whose standing both in Jewish affairs and in the larger American society was of high order.

Jonah was tapped on the shoulder for the assignment of originating a program and running it. Warburg would have no one else. In three years of association with Jonah in the JDC, the central agency for overseas Jewish relief, he had come to marvel at the rabbi's human instinct, breadth of sympathy, common touch, and absorption with the American dream, combined with energy, humor, and

organizing ability—just the qualities needed for this particular job.

Jonah was already recognized as a master publicist,
but his previous direct experience with the radio medium,
although of some length of standing, was of the most
casual sort. In the days when headphone-wearing radio
buffs assembled their own crystal sets and stayed up until
daybreak for the excitement of logging stations two or three
hundred miles away, he had attended sessions of the "hoot
owls," a zany group of Portland businessmen who got together around a microphone and let off steam. Charles
Berg, one of Jonah's more intimate cronies, had been one of
the leading spirits of the group. Whether that experience of
the early 1920s had any lasting influence on Jonah is hard
to say; but he was a man who tucked away every scrap of
unused experience for possible use at some future date.

NBC acceded to Jonah's request for a Saturday program (better suited to a Jewish broadcast than the Sunday
choice of the *Catholic Hour* and the *National Radio Pulpit*) and
gave the *Message of Israel* a weekly half-hour of prime time—
Saturday night at six, almost the best on the air. Time of
that order was a rarer gift than gold. The *Message* kept its
choice Saturday-evening spot until 1950, when it was advanced to 10 o'clock Sunday morning.

The half-hour unit—the general preference for religious
programs from 1931 on—imposed upon the *Message* the
fortunate necessity of simplicity, directness, and perfect
timing. Radio listeners are the least captive of audiences,
and, when called upon to exercise patience, switch to another station instead. The *Message* soon acquired a consist-
ently loyal audience and was not often subjected to this
indignity. The brief, tight program had wide popular

appeal. Its continued existence was greeted with a steady stream of unsolicited fan mail. Later on, when listener reaction was tested—for example, when discs of liturgical music recorded by the Central Synagogue musical ensemble were made available free for the asking—the response was extremely lively.

Separately and together, the religious broadcasts over the early radio networks were a major force in interfaith understanding. All reached huge audiences, which crossed sectarian boundaries. Under the circumstances, good manners, if nothing else, dictated avoidance of proselytizing, dogmatizing, or criticism of any sect or denomination. The programs, however, went further than mere observance of such restraints, and consciously developed messages that were universal in conception and appeal. They were, accordingly, universally accepted. In a country that had more than thirty times as many Christians as Jews in it, the *Message of Israel*, not unnaturally, had many more Christian than Jewish listeners. Jonah had his non-Jewish listeners very much in mind when he shaped his broadcasts, for it was important as never before that American Christians see their Jewish neighbors for what they were.

Quotations from two letters, both written in the 1950s but much like thousands of others received throughout Jonah's 25-year-long radio ministry, are revealing for the rapport that they show established between the *Message* and its non-Jewish listeners:

It was the singing of that choir that first attracted me to the program. Off and on for weeks, months, I had twisted dials on Sunday morning in hope of finding some "satisfying music" but no luck; then suddenly, there it was—exactly what I had been searching for and missing probably by seconds. Beautiful, satisfying music, beautifully sung by really excellent voices. To think I had been missing it right along!

I was slightly amused to learn that it was a "Jewish service" —expecting to hear a lot of informative ritual—but it could have been a service from my own church. I enjoyed the speakers too, although I usually steer clear of all speakers, except, perhaps, our President. I have grown to love the voice of Rabbi Jonah B. Wise, and miss him greatly when he is away.

Many of the anthems sung by the Temple choir are sung by our own choir—such as "Sanctus," "Lift Thine Eyes," "Bless The Lord, O My Soul."   E. T.

*   *   *

This letter is prompted by your rather lonely comment a couple of weeks ago to the effect that you do not know much about your listening audience, its size and its reaction to your program.

I don't know much about it either, aside from the fact that my husband and I listen regularly and we have discovered much to our surprise that several of our friends also listen. I speak of it as a surprise because, you see, none of us are Jewish. Now when you are a Scotch Presbyterian it is a little awkward to casually refer to what Rabbi So-&-So said on the Message of Israel, and yet that has happened, and it happened because what is said on your program is not only applicable but quotable.

What is it that we like? The reasoned, almost intellectualized approach. The short description of Jewish holidays, what they are and why (which have always been a mystery before). The happy relief from "hell fire and damnation" and the raving and/or groaning of preachers. In short, you and your special speakers are worth listening to, for information, guidance, and, if you like, for understanding. And more than that, the program is stimulating—after the series "We Wrote the Bible" (which was a little annoying) my husband stormed out the next day and bought the new revised Bible and he is reading it from cover to cover. He is now about halfway through; has recovered from his original anger; and he acts like a small boy who has just discovered a roomful of wonderful new toys. All evening long it is "Hey, listen to this!" or "I bet you didn't know...."

You have given us a new world to explore—a very exciting experience. Please don't become discouraged because your audience does not write—it is difficult to know what to say except to thank you.   B.R.D.

Perhaps the greatest tribute to the impact of the *Message* emerged as the *Message To Israel*, a program by means of which, in 1944, a Mr. Shepard of Atlantic City sought to convert the Jews. Its name invaded the copyright by which the name "Message of Israel" was protected. But it was otherwise conducted on a reasonably high plane, and Jonah had no inclination to provide it with the amplification of legal action. He therefore did nothing at all about the *Message To Israel*, which goes on as before, undeterred by the less-than-impressive size of its radio audience.

The comparative popularity of the sermons broadcast by the *Message of Israel* during its first fifteen years was measured in a study performed in 1950. The sole criterion was the volume of mail received. Among the five sermons drawing the most mail—3000 letters or more—four, interestingly enough, dealt with the relationship of Judaism and Christianity. The most popular—by Rabbi Ferdinand Isserman of Temple Israel, St. Louis—was "The Jewish Jesus and the Christian Christ," which produced a yield of 5000 letters. Then, in descending order, came "Christianity's Debt to Judaism," "The Jewish Position on Jesus," and "Judaism's Debt to Christianity." In fifth place was "Wise Rules for a Happy Marriage," the best-drawing sermon in the second most popular category: the religious approach to life problems.

Most of the guest speakers were Jonah's colleagues in the Reform rabbinate; among those who appeared most frequently in prewar years were Barnett Brickner, Abraham Feinberg, Solomon Freehof, Roland Gittelsohn, Morris Lazaron, Joshua Liebman, Louis Mann, Louis Newman, Irving Reichert, Hyman Schachtel, and Louis Wolsey. An Orthodox rabbi, David de Sola Pool of New York's Spanish-Portuguese Synagogue, also put in many appearances. The guest speaker producing the greatest spontaneous volume of mail and financial contributions to the *Massage* was the psychiatric-oriented Rabbi Joshua Loth Liebman of Boston, author of *Peace of Mind*, who appeared often during the 1940s. Nonclerical guest speakers were few. Notable among these in the *Message's* early years were John Dewey, the distinguished philosopher; Albert Einstein; William Kilpatrick of Teachers College, Columbia, philosopher of education; and Mary Woolley, peace advocate and president of Mount Holyoke College.

The eloquence of the *Message* was due in no little part to its splendid music under the direction of Frederick Lechner, who was also the soloist. Lechner was assisted by Alexander Richardson, organist, and Lazar Weiner, a liturgical composer of note as well as choirmaster. In style of work, Lechner was Jonah's opposite. Jonah, although never late for a broadcast, sometimes showed up rather later than he should have—far too late for his musical director's happiness and comfort. A minute or two later, while his fellow performers were still pulling themselves together after their bout with anxiety, he would begin the program with unshaken composure. His radio sermons, delivered from notes, were casual and unrehearsed; their spontaneity had much to do with their appeal. Lechner, on the other hand, left nothing to the vagary of the moment. His music was planned and put together like a fine watch; and the performers were drilled and rehearsed until Jonah would get fretful. "Stop singing!" he would say. "Stop rehearsing! Since when do professional musicians have to rehearse?" "Amateurs don't have to," Lechner would reply. "The greater the artist, the more he rehearses."

From time to time, Jonah and Lechner would tangle over guest artists. Lechner was perfectly content to have such musically accomplished guests as the Jewish choir of West Point, but exhibited signs of rebellion when Jonah scheduled the Central Synagogue children's choir. Jonah liked to hear childish voices once in a while, and thought the audience did, too; Lechner objected to any lapse from the *Message*'s lofty standard of performance. In most confrontations with Lechner, Jonah ended up by bowing to his colleague's professional judgment. But the children had put in many faithful hours of choir practice and were entitled to the reward—his to bestow—of being allowed to appear on the *Message*. Here Jonah overruled Lechner. He was more flexible with him in differences over other aspects of programing. "Look at other programs," he would say to Lechner. "See the use they make of simple hymns, familiar hymns. Why cut ourselves off from a bigger audience? There are people, lots of them, who want the religious music of their childhood. They're looking for it; let them have it. Isn't it our duty?" "Our duty," Lechner would reply, "is to improve religious music in America. We are leaders. We are educators." Jonah would then throw up his hands in something very close to despair. "Oh! What an idealist you are!"

The hard work behind putting on a show every week

was considerable, and grew with the ever-increasing number of participating stations. At first, managerial chores
were in the care of Saul Applebaum, who, in the 1930s, was
Jonah's assistant rabbi at Central Synagogue as well as his
radio manager at the Jewish Layman's Committee. Applebaum moved on to another post in 1941, and Jonah
prevailed upon his own son David, who had been a schoolteacher in Portland for several years, but had just returned
to the East, to take over the management of the *Message*.

Over the past 25 years, David Wise has been program
director, except during his wartime service in the armed
forces. He now both produces the show and acts as its host.
In 1949, the Union of American Hebrew Congregations
became cosponsor with the Layman's Committee—thereby
making the *Message* the official radio voice of Reform
Judaism—and the following year David became the director of radio and television for the UAHC. In that capacity,
he founded the *Temple Hour*, a nationally broadcast religious radio service heard every week since 1950, *Design for
Living*, a weekly program broadcast heard in New York,
from 1950 to 1955, and helped produce the series *Adventures
in Judaism*. He also created the program *Song of Israel*, using
the Central Synagogue choir, for Station WMCA, New
York. Both the *Message* and the *Temple Hour*, through his
efforts, were taken up by the Armed Forces Radio Service
and rebroadcast all over the world. After Jonah's death the
programs were taped and no longer transmitted live.

In 1950, at the laying of the cornerstone of UAHC's
new building on Fifth Avenue, where the *Message* now has
its headquarters, Jonathan Wise, the three-year-old son of
David, grandson of Jonah, and great-grandson of Isaac
Mayer, was given a conspicuous part in the ceremony, thus

visibly linking four generations of Wises in a continuing tradition of service to and in behalf of Reform Judaism in America.

· VII ·

The JDC and the UJA

O N A HILL NEAR THE EDGE OF JERUSALEM stands one of the world's strangest monuments. There, rooms of flame and smoke are succeeded by other rooms whose stone walls are inscribed with thousands upon thousands of names. They are not the names of individual men and women but the names of Jewish communities—villages, towns, and cities of Austria, Czechoslovakia, Germany, Hungary, Poland, and Romania with Jewish populations ranging from a few dozen to the Warsaw ghetto's 450,000 (in 1943). With the Jewish communities of Russia, they constituted one self-contained civilization with a history stretching sixteen hundred years into the past. All are now nothing but a memory. Of the seven million Jews who inhabited them, six million were killed in Hitler's murder camps. More than half of the million who survived were saved from extinction by a man-made miracle, the American Jewish Joint Distribution Committee—the JDC.

What the Jews of America did for the surviving Jews of Central Europe had once been done for them. Seventy-five

years ago, driven by a fury of Russian and Romanian pogroms, a terrified and destitute Jewish multitude stampeded
westward. The Jews of Central and Western Europe,
through the Alliance Israelite Universelle, provided the
funds and administration to regulate that disorganized
flight and channel it into resettlement in newer lands
across the sea. Between 1880 and 1914, 2,500,000 of those
emigrants came to the United States, where the established
American Jewish community was swamped by the task of
caring for newcomers who outnumbered them eight to one.
The American Jewish leaders appealed to Europe for help,
which was accorded at once and on a great scale. The contributions of one donor, Baron Maurice de Hirsch, the
German Jew who built Turkey's railroad system, amounted
to $40 million, which he divided between North and South
America. We can only wonder how many Eastern European Jews would have been absorbed here without aid
from their coreligionists in Germany, Austria, Hungary,
France, and England—certainly nothing like 2,500,000.
The aid so freely given turned out to be a spectacularly
successful investment, for it became the turn of America's
Jews—most of whom were the children and grandchildren
of refugees—to rescue Jews of Europe.

The overseas rescue, relief, and reconstruction activities
of the JDC during and after two wars are related with
economy, passion, and grace in Herbert Agar's remarkable
book, *The Saving Remnant*. The story of the American activities that made those overseas activities possible—largely
fund raising and administration—has yet to be told. That
work, however, received from the men responsible for it
the same full measure of effort, devotion, and resourceful-
ness as the operations in Europe and Israel received from

the JDC's overseas staff. In this service, Jonah B. Wise was *primus inter pares*—first among equals—and performed his gigantic task with such self-deprecating modesty and humor as to disguise the dimensions of his contribution. From 1930 until his death in 1959, he was vice-chairman of the JDC and national chairman of fund raising; and for the twenty years following the 1939 merger of JDC fund raising with the United Palestine Appeal in the United Jewish Appeal, he was national chairman of the UJA, in which he represented the JDC.

In 1930 Jonah accepted the chairmanship of the 1931 national JDC campaign upon the invitation of Felix M. Warburg, the retired JDC chairman, and Paul Baerwald, the chairman. Warburg, perhaps the most distinguished figure among American Jews, was seeking a replacement for Rabbi Judah Magnes in the councils of the JDC. Magnes had performed a brilliant fund-raising job during World War I, after which he had gone to Jerusalem to become the first chancellor of the Hebrew University. Jonah was eminently qualified for his new assignment, not only by his gift for organization and his virtuoso skills in bending people to his will, but also by college training and near-professional experience in community work. In addition, his yeoman service on behalf of West Coast fund-raising drives had attracted more than a little notice in the New York headquarters of Jewish relief and rehabilitation organizations during and after World War I. He was brought to Warburg's notice by I. Edwin Goldwasser, the longtime unpaid treasurer of the JDC, and Rabbi Solomon Lowenstein, his old friend from Hebrew Union College days, who, in 1930, was the able head of the New York Federation of Jewish Philanthropies.

Jonah, through his chairmanship of fund raising, was a member of the JDC executive committee. In addition, he became a member of the administrative committee, the smaller group that ran the organization during the intervals between executive meetings. The executive committee met in the Warburg mansion on upper Fifth Avenue in a beautiful room hung with Rembrandt etchings. The administrative committee, which included Felix Warburg, Paul Baerwald, Moses Leavitt, James N. Rosenberg, and Jonah B. Wise, usually met at lunch or at the JDC offices in midtown New York.

A close friendship developed between Jonah and Felix Warburg—and indeed, with the entire Warburg family. Warburg never got over the nonrabbinical aspect of his new colleague—the brisk manner, the homburg, the trim business suit, the passion for gardening, bridge, and golf—for all the world the attributes of a corporation lawyer or Wall Street broker. Neither, for that matter, did Warburg's wife, the former Frieda Schiff. After twenty-five years of close acquaintance, she still scolded Jonah for his lack of sacerdotal dignity and tried to reform him even in his seventies, when he was a neighbor in Hartsdale and frequently dropped in with his grandchildren to pay her a visit. The younger Warburgs, although he was their father's associate, found him their own contemporary in spirit. Edward M. M. Warburg, the present chairman of the JDC, was, in 1930, a senior at Harvard. His interest in the JDC was aroused when he was home during college vacations and heard discussions between Jonah Wise and Felix Warburg. He soon came under Jonah's spell and joined the Central Synagogue, where, he felt, religion was presented in all purity, untainted by tribalism or ritualistic trappings. Even here, Jonah would continually test his younger friend with his own special brand of shock treatment. When his friend congratulated him on a particularly effective sermon, he would answer, characteristically, "Why, Eddie! That was No. 18!" Actually, Jonah sometimes prepared a sermon, but, once in the pulpit, he would abandon his text for a complete improvisation. When Edward's daughter Daphne was born, Jonah gave Edward a cutting from one of his daphne bushes brought to New York from Portland—Mr. Warburg now has a clump of bushes grown from the original plant. It is rumored that Jonah, when he performed the marriage ceremony over Paul and Jean Warburg in California, played Paul a round of golf for the fee.

In 1930, the nation was plunging deep into depression; and the American Jewish community, occupied with its own severe economic problems, looked with some disfavor on providing funds for the remaining Jewish sufferers from the dislocation in Eastern Europe—primarily Poland and Romania—following World War I. Less than $1,000,000 was made available for overseas distribution in 1931, and this figure dropped to $375,000 the next year. Under those circumstances, the question arose whether the JDC program in Eastern Europe might not well be discontinued altogether. James N. Rosenberg, president of the American Society for Jewish Farm Settlements in Russia as well as of Agro-Joint (the JDC arm that settled 300,000 Jews on Crimean land contributed by the Soviet government), made a tour of investigation through Poland and Romania to determine whether the condition of the Eastern European Jews would permit the winding up of the JDC. He was horrified by the privation and misery he found everywhere. The Jews, the most exposed and precariously situated members of Eastern European society generally, had been the first to suffer the heavy blows of world-wide depression. There was no discontinuance of American support. "We can't," said Mr. Rosenberg on his return.

There were only a few JDC staff members to direct fund raising for the entire United States and Canada. There were exactly two to go out into the field: Jonah and his newly appointed professional fund-raising director, Isidor Coons, both of whom traveled far and wide to keep the JDC alive.

"Dor" Coons, editor of the *Wilkes-Barre Evening News* until he became an army officer in World War I, was a personal representative of Herbert Hoover in the postwar National Collection of the European Relief Council. The term of his appointment in 1930 was six months but it was nineteen years and $535 million dollars later before he actually said good-by. For ten of those years, 1939 to 1949, he was executive vice-chairman of the UJA national campaign. He may be regarded, in Edward M. M. Warburg's words, as "a prime architect of the present UJA fund-raising structure through which millions of human beings have been given hope and a new chance in life."

A close and affectionate relation grew between Jonah and his younger colleague as the two men developed into a smoothly working team. A smoothly working team after 8.30 a.m., that is—for, until he had had his cup of coffee in the morning, Jonah, who was a bad sleeper, would brook the company of no one. All fund-raising committees in the communities to which Jonah traveled were warned by Coons to send no welcoming delegation before nine o'clock in the morning; a most disconcerting experience awaited any delegation so foolhardy as to disobey those instructions. "Tell me," said Coons to Helen Wise shortly after he had begun to assist her husband, "does Jonah have breakfast with you at home?" She sighed. "Ah," she replied, "you have found that out already." Once Jonah had risen from the breakfast table and was ready to face the world, he and Coons were the most congenial of companions. He not only respected Coons's ability and dedication, but took the interest of an older brother in seeing that he was happy in his chosen career. The two traveled incessantly, separately and together, and the work brought many strains; yet neither ever delivered a harsh word to the other.

With Coons by Jonah's side, the important business of reorganizing the JDC fund-raising program proceeded carefully but with all due speed. Gradually, a revitalized network of committees for financial solicitation was built all over the United States. Jonah had amply demonstrated his capacity to organize on many previous occasions, but never before had it been so important that he call on every ounce of organizing skill that he possessed. In doing the job, he acquitted himself magnificently. It is questionable whether anyone else could have done it quite so well.

At least locally in New York, Jonah spent a good deal of time going to small neighborhood groups, and, once in a while, would run into some unexpected reactions:

"Tell Mr. Warburg *he* should give $100."

"You don't talk so good like Stephen Wise."

Resistance toward giving dwindled as need increased abroad and understanding at home. Hitler, in 1931 and 1932, became a menace to reckon with, although most political leaders and analysts still regarded him as a tem-

porary phenomenon, too freakish and deranged ever to
be accorded power by the great German people. Among
the people on the scene who did not so deceive themselves
was Dr. Bernhard Kahn of Berlin, the European director
of the JDC and a most diligent and careful observer. His
grim confidential reports were delivered to attentive listeners. Both Jonah B. Wise and Felix Warburg, let it be
said, were, early in 1931, genuinely alive to the Hitler
menace and aware that desperate efforts would be needed
to mitigate its disastrous effect upon Jewish life in Germany.
Neither could foretell how complete the disaster would be,
nor could anyone; but Jonah was aware of the deep, dark
recesses within the German soul, despite his admiration
for German culture. During his *Wanderjahr*, as we saw in
Chapter 3, he had been moved to send home a news essay
on the pervasiveness and depth of German antisemitism.
Moreover, his highly developed sense of history enabled
him to gauge the amplitude and direction of movements
and the significance of events with clarity and objectivity.
Accordingly, the JDC prepared for what its leaders thought
would be the worst—although the actual worst proved
almost beyond human imagining.

Hitler became Chancellor in 1933, and the great work
of rescue and resettlement of German Jews began. In this
work, the JDC gained the active co-operation of the South
African Jewish Appeal; the United Jewish Refugee & War
Relief Agencies, Canada; the Central British Fund; the
Junta de Aguda pro Victimas de la Guerra, Argentina;
United Jewish Overseas Relief Fund, Australia; Compañia
Unida Reconstruccion Aguda, Mexico; and other organi-
zations. Two months after Hitler came to power, Jonah
was in Germany to confer with German Jewish community

leaders and find out their most urgent needs. He was the first prominent American Jew to go to Hitlerland, and there were many who feared for his safety. Jonah, however, did not feel that he was in danger, and, in any case, was a man utterly without fear. He paid no heed to those who tried to dissuade him, and he went. More remarkable, perhaps, he was undaunted by the rigors of his ocean crossing, which was so stormy that he had to wedge himself between his washstand and dresser in order to shave. Most of the passengers took to their bunks, but Jonah was on hand for every meal.

The German Jewish leaders were divided in assessing their plight. "We, too, are Germans," said some, "and have been living with these other Germans for a long time. We will all work things out in our own way." And others: "Hitler's measures are not being directed against us, the truly German Jews, but only against the Jews from Poland, Lithuania, Russia, and Romania who have migrated here since the war and have frightened the Germans by their numbers and antagonized them by their unacceptable ways. Soon the situation will be stabilized, and everything will be all right." But Leo Baeck, President of the Union of German Rabbis, knew that the future had closed shut for the Jews of Germany. "I will stay here with my people," he said to Jonah.[1] "This is where I belong. But save the next generation of German Jews. Get the Jews out of

---

[1]In 1936, Baeck conducted a group of Jewish children to safety in England. He then went back to Germany. His return was in no way intended as a dramatic sacrificial gesture; he wanted to provide some comfort to his fellow German Jews in their extremity, and help them meet a bleak future with courage and composure. During the war, he knew the horrors of concentration camp life. Surviving them, he spent the last ten years of his life in the United States, where he was a faculty member of Hebrew Union College.

Germany, especially the young." Jonah reported back to
New York that the end had come for Germany's Jews.
They would have to be brought out.

The drive for funds was accelerated. In 1932, the JDC
had $375,000 to expend on its overseas program; in 1938,
it had $4 million. With Jonah doing the planning and
almost every American Jewish leader actively joining in
to ensure the success of this crucially important enterprise,
the nationwide fund-raising network took on new firmness
and density. Jonah personally concentrated on meeting
with the leaders of America's twelve largest metropolitan
areas—New York, Chicago, Los Angeles, Cleveland, Baltimore, Boston, Philadelphia, and so forth. As often as he
could, he also visited other communities with substantial
Jewish populations—Columbus, Atlanta, Milwaukee, Albany, Kansas City, and scores of others. The smaller centers
to be covered were so numerous that it would have taken
an army of field men to visit them all. Jonah, therefore,
recruited volunteer fund solicitors by mail. He drafted each
letter himself, and almost every one he sent brought grati-
fying results. Surprisingly, he was able to smoke out responsible local leadership in this way, and, thus, from a distance,
to establish regional setups and make possible a large
decentralized fund-raising effort. Each region held an annual small-town leaders' meeting at which Jonah was the
principal speaker.

The *Message of Israel* was not overlooked as a possible aid
to the JDC. Along with information about the condition of
the Jews in Europe, Jonah regularly broadcasted the story
of the JDC to millions of Jews and Christians, receiving a
steady stream of financial contributions from members of
all faiths.

Attending meeting after meeting week after week, Jonah made a legion of friends for the JDC. This accomplishment was, later, translated into moral and financial support. The fund-raising network expanded; in 1938, the year in which JDC fund raising was merged into the UJA, it included 3000 communities in the United States. That number continued to grow after the merger; in 1948, it totaled 5000.

Jonah recognized that an organization created in 1914 had aging leadership a quarter-century later. He took account of the need to create new interest and leadership through enlisting the young in positions of responsibility. Edward M. M. Warburg gave early and complete commitment, becoming, first, chairman of the New York area of the JDC, and, in 1941, national chairman; he also became cochairman of the UJA in 1939, and national chairman in 1951. Pauline Baerwald—now Mrs. Myron K. Falk, Jr.—daughter of Paul Baerwald, was still in her twenties when she organized the JDC Youth Division, which she established on a national basis as an educational and fund-raising arm of the senior organization.

In his personal efforts of recruiting and fund raising, Jonah was particularly effective among small groups, where his ready wit, easy manner, and unique ability to tell a good story caught his audiences and held them. Here he showed himself to better advantage than in the pulpit, where he was sometimes a little stiff and ill at ease. He knew how profound was the Jewish sense of charitable obligation and never tried to promote participation in the work of rescue solely on the basis of pity for the unfortunate. Rather, he stressed the responsibility of American Jews as the largest, richest, and freest segment of world Jewry. His

presentations were always statesmanlike exercises in information and education rather than mere persuasion—the
bare facts were more persuasive than anything anyone
could say. His technique was always the same, and it was
as simple as it was devastatingly effective. First he leveled
his hearers' defenses with a few well-placed anecdotes, and
when they could no longer resist him he told them what
had to be done. Jonah knew his own people. Once aware
of the mounting plight of their brethren across the seas—
for, with hundreds of refugees arriving in America every
week, they could not help but be aware—they responded
with a mounting self-imposed taxation unprecedented in
history.

Three heavy blows fell upon Europe's Jews in 1938.
They manifestly ushered in a new era of entrapment and
oppression.

The first was the Anschluss, in which Hitler took over
Austria, with its Jewish population of 200,000. Perhaps
75,000 Jews had escaped from Germany by the first months
of 1938, so that more Jews were being held captive than in
1933, the year in which the persecutions began. Millions
of other Jews in Czechoslovakia, Poland, and Hungary were
aware that, some day soon, insult, imprisonment, mutila-
tion, and death were coming.

The second was the failure of the international conference at Evian, France, which had been called by President Roosevelt to consider which nations would accept
refugees from Germany. Jonah attended the conference as
a delegate from the United States. Much sympathy was
expressed for the German refugees at Evian, but no nation
anywhere would take them, except—almost incredibly—
the Dominican Republic. A handful of refugees went there,

and a colony was established at Sosúa. The colonists put
down no roots in Sosúa, where they lived from day to day
in the hope that ultimately they could go to North or South
America. On his return from Evian, Jonah reported immediately to all the metropolitan and regional JDC leaders
in the United States. He went in person to larger cities and
sent letters to small communities. About $1 million in
emergency funds was raised by this mid-campaign appeal.

The third and greatest blow was the "night of broken
glass"—Kristall Nacht, November 10. All over Germany
and Austria, SS men launched a concerted attack upon
the Jews at 2 o'clock in the morning. Synagogues were
burned down; homes were gutted; personal possessions
were seized; inmates were evicted from hospitals and welfare institutions; men, women, and children were hunted,
beaten, and killed. A few days later, male Jews were
rounded up and sent into "protective" custody for several
weeks; from this protection 35,000 never returned. All Jews
were excluded from schools and public places.

Kristall Nacht was followed by a decisive change in
American fund raising for Jewish overseas relief.

For several years, the Central British Fund for German
Jewry had urged the formation of an international council
to include both the JDC and the United Palestine Appeal.
The JDC top leadership contributed work and money to
this project. It found itself also working with such American
Zionists as Rabbi Stephen S. Wise, many of whose purposes
it did not share. The JDC executive was composed almost
entirely of men who adhered strictly to the classical Reform
proposition that the Jews constituted a religious body, not
a nation; those men were opposed on principle to support
of Jewish nationalism. They were not unwilling—they were

in fact eager—to assist in sending German refugees to Palestine. In doing so, however, they insisted on avoiding the appearance, the name, and the substance of Zionism. A crisis had arisen in 1938, when it had been proposed that the JDC and the United Palestine Appeal get together in a single fund-raising effort. Patently, a combined effort would raise the most money in the most efficient way; on this basis, it was supported by some members of the JDC executive. Jonah was not among them. He was opposed to Zionism and opposed even more to a plan that seemed to thrust Zionism down the throats of American non-Zionists and anti-Zionists. He argued vigorously against the proposed merger. So did James N. Rosenberg, and, on November 9, the JDC executive committee voted "No" to a united appeal. But, within twenty-four hours, the full fury of Kristall Nacht was unleashed.

Now everything was changed. There were no longer strategic questions about how European Jews should be brought out or where refuge should be sought. They had to to brought out by any means possible and sent anywhere they could go. The only issue was survival.

The extremity of the crisis rendered disunity a luxury that the American Jews could no longer afford. Overnight, the question of Zionism became secondary. Wise and Rosenberg both withdrew their objections to pooling efforts with the United Palestine Appeal. In 1939, with the JDC and the United Palestine Appeal as constituent agencies, the UJA—the United Jewish Appeal—became a reality. In the next quarter-century it was to raise $1.5 billion! The JDC had $8 million to spend in 1939; in 1947—its peak year—it had $70 million. With Rabbi Abba Hillel Silver of the United Palestine Appeal, Jonah became national chairman of the new organization; Coons became one of the two executive vice-chairmen. Although until he died he never accepted Zionism, Jonah became an unwavering friend and supporter of Israel.

The eight months before the outbreak of war on September 1, 1939 witnessed a heroic job of lifesaving. Nearly 135,000 desperate Jews—88,000 from Germany, the rest from other countries—were helped to flee the Continent before the trap shut tight. The largest number, 75,000, went to England, where immigration restrictions were waived and the English people, Jews and gentiles alike, willingly became sponsors for the plundered and hunted German, Austrian, and Czechoslovakian refugees. Not quite half so many went to Palestine, through the efforts of the United Palestine Appeal, and 25,000 came to the United States, where the National Refugee Service (later the United Service for New Americans), an affiliate of the JDC under the chairmanship of William Rosenwald, assisted in their rehabilitation.

After the outbreak of war, Europe became a slaughterhouse for the Jews left behind; and the next six years were a nightmare of massacres, tortures, so-called medical experiments, murder camps, gas chambers, and crematories. By trickles and spurts, 125,000 escaped or were rescued, many of them by the Haganah, the underground military organization of the Jews in Palestine, which sent daring young men and women—"the boys"—into occupied Europe to snatch Jews away from under the noses of the Nazis. Eight hundred thousand more were spared, the greater number of them because the rapid envelopment of Nazi-held territory upset the schedule of killings, but some through the last-minute attempt by defeated Nazi leaders to win leniency from the Allies. Late in the war, President Roosevelt established the War Refugee Board, headed by Secretary of the Treasury Henry Morgenthau, which enabled the JDC to convert funds and send money into enemy territory. From European headquarters directed by Dr. Joseph Schwartz in neutral Lisbon, the JDC maintained an active field organization—mostly underground—of 42 offices and more than a hundred agents. The necessities of life were provided for hundreds of thousands of persons. How many lives were saved by this work we shall never know.

By the end of the war, Hitler's ambition to "solve" the Jewish problem had come close to being realized. The problems of the few Jews left seemed well-nigh insoluble. The French, Belgian, Dutch, and Italian Jews could return to their own countries. But the rest—naked, sick, starving, homeless—had nowhere to go. America would take only a few, in accordance with immigration laws. Indeed, the DP Act passed by the Eightieth Congress in 1948 was crudely discriminatory toward Jews. The British, fearing Arab wrath and the possible loss of major sources of oil, would let only a handful into Palestine. As early as 1939, the British government issued its well-known White Paper on the subject of Jewish immigration: only 75,000 entry certificates were to be issued before the establishment of Palestine as an Arab-controlled state, and noncertificated immigration was to be "illegal." The Jewish Agency for Palestine was not consulted—as it had to be under Article 6 of the League of Nations Mandate—and insisted that the White Paper was itself "illegal." The European lands east of the Rhine were a hated world charged with intolerable memories and were savagely, murderously antisemitic (as the Poles promptly demonstrated in the Kielce pogrom, which was launched against hapless Jews who had returned from the Soviet Union to their former homes). The Crimean homes of the 800,000 Jews settled by Agro-Joint were ashes and ruins. Their former occupants had been obliterated. Jews could not go back to those ghostlands to place their lives in jeopardy again. Nor could they stay herded behind the barbed wire of the wretched, crowded, and unsanitary DP camps in the American, British, and French zones of Germany, where the Jewish populations continued to grow while non-Jewish DPs were being repatriated by the millions.

The Jewish instinct for survival, rekindled by liberation, now flamed out against the efforts of the postwar world to provide partial, unexamined, and unacceptable solutions to the problem of what place in the scheme of things could be found for the tortured remnant of Europe's Jews. The DPs refused to place themselves at the disposal of a Western world that, no matter how well-intentioned, had done so little to save them from the Nazi fury and was now so little inclined to enable them to build life anew. They were determined, live or die, to be with their own people in their own land, and to take charge of their own destiny. Their aspirations for a renewed Jewish life in Palestine and nowhere but Palestine were "an arrow of longing, yearning for the opposite shore." While still in the DP camps, they formed a "government" of their own, the truculent Central Committee of Liberated Jews, which prepared the most resolute and concentrated of the numerous migrations in Jewish history.

As the war years themselves had been, the immediate postwar years were a period of struggle between the Jewish

Agency and the British government, an undeclared war in which the Jewish Agency did everything in its power to bring Jews to Palestine and the British government everything in its power to keep them out. Hardly any Jewish organization recognized the legality of the British exclusion policy—which, as noted, was in contravention of the mandate from the League of Nations. Determination was high to settle the DPs in Palestine without respect to British opposition and to arm the Haganah against all eventualities.

In December 1945, called together by Rabbi James G. Heller, William Rosenwald, and Rabbi Jonah B. Wise, national chairmen, the UJA community leaders from all over the United States met at Atlantic City. Heading the agenda was the question of what emergency measures could match the expanding and accelerating need for money. In the year then ending, the UJA had asked the Jews of America to contribute on the basis of a one-time sacrificial appeal never to be repeated. The sum of $35 million had been raised—the maximum possible, everyone had thought. But the UJA had miscalculated the need. Now, at Atlantic City, the unheard-of goal of $100 million was set for the UJA's 1946 "survival" year. Not only was the JDC obligated to rehabilitate the Jewish survivors in Europe and to assist the United Palestine Appeal in transporting them to Palestine—a mostly noncertificated migration, and therefore perilous and expensive—but also to provide relief for Jews in Arab-populated North Africa, which, toward the end of 1945, had exploded in a series of pogroms.

Could $100 million be raised in 1946? That goal was exceeded: $101 million was raised. And, in 1947, $117 million. Sixty per cent, the usual proportion, was turned over to the JDC.

Between 1945 and 1947, 56,000 immigrants entered Palestine, 80 per cent of them illegals, and an almost identical number was admitted into the United States. All those immigrants were assisted by the JDC, both along the way and after reaching their destinations.

The figures for Palestine represented a notable success in the battle for migration launched by the Jewish Agency with co-operation from all other Zionist bodies. The Haganah—now trained to thwart the British by the British general Orde Wingate—was the driving force in this battle. Its men were everywhere, selecting emigrants, conducting them to embarkation centers, chartering ships, and leading organized resistance to British marines when the ships were intercepted by British naval vessels. Between 1945 and 1947, more than two score Haganah ships were crammed with refugees and sent across the Mediterranean. Many ships were caught and their passengers dragged off, but only after a melée in which bottles and sticks were opposed to the machine guns, carbines, and truncheons of the British. The internment camps in Haifa and Cyprus were the scenes of further resistance, hunger strikes, and severe punishments by camp authorities. The refugees were ready to be killed rather than go back to Europe, and acted with corresponding desperation.

The climax came when the *Exodus 1947* was rammed three times, machine-gunned, and brought to Haifa. Its 4500 passengers, reloaded in three ships, were returned to France, whence they had sailed but where they now refused to disembark. The three ships then sailed to Germany, where the passengers were removed, after a three-hour-long bloody fight, and thrown into concentration camps. The outcry over this incident was world-wide.

The bitter tactics of the Jews would hardly have succeeded against the Nazis, who would have killed them all
without turning a hair. The British were not Nazis, however, and, furthermore, were divided in their feelings.
They threw up their hands. They announced that they
were giving up the Mandate; and, in November 1947, the
UN resolved to partition Palestine into a Jewish and an
Arab state. In May 1948, the British took their leave, and
Ben Gurion proclaimed "the establishment of a Jewish
state in Palestine to be called 'Israel.'" Not only did the
DPs dare to hope again, but hope was coming very close
to palpable reality. There were no more restrictions on
immigration. In 1948, 115,000 DPs poured into Israel,
aided by the joint efforts of the JDC and the United
Palestine Appeal.

The Arab nations surrounding Israel did not accept
partition. They meant Palestine to have a single administration and that, Arab. In a bid to strangle Israel at its
birth, they attacked immediately with 25,000 troops supported by planes and tanks. The 5000 men of the Haganah,
swelled to 10,000 by volunteers, were equipped with little
more than carbines and machine guns. But they were veterans of years of fighting against Rommel and the Afrika
Korps under Alexander and Montgomery, and were
awesomely competent at desert warfare. In a few short
weeks, they drove the Arabs well beyond the borders drawn
by the UN. The Arabs, their numbers raised to 150,000,
attacked twice again. But meanwhile the Haganah had
also become much larger, and, in spite of an arms embargo
decreed by the Security Council, American Flying Fortresses, British tanks, and Czech small arms had been sped
to Israel. Both attacks were quickly defeated. The survivors

of the European catastrophe now had not only earned a homeland but a sense of pride in heroic accomplishment.

In 1948, the UJA asked the Jews of the United States to contribute far more heavily than ever before. This was the "Year of Destiny" campaign, which raised $160 million. The twelve large metropolitan centers gave eight times as much as they had in 1939, the UJA's first year; the seventeen next largest gave fourteen times as much; the smaller centers thirteen times as much; and the country as a whole ten times as much. The money raised averaged out to $125 for every Jewish family in America.

The peak years of giving and spending, 1947 and 1948, were followed by a year of lesser though still extraordinary money-raising effort. Vast new funds were required in 1949 to assist the Jews of the Near East. Always submerged and poverty-stricken, afflicted with malaria, trachoma, and tuberculosis, they were now on the verge of annihilation. The anger of the defeated and frustrated Arab nations had been turned upon them with extreme harshness, and they were denied the opportunity to earn a livelihood.

Once again, Jews by the scores and hundreds of thousands needed food, medical care, training for a new life, and transportation to a place of security. Through "Operation Magic Carpet," some 50,000 Yemenite Jews were flown 1500 miles to Israel from Aden in 1949 and 1950. At the same time, 150,000 more refugees arrived from the DP camps in Germany. In 1965, the year of this writing, hundreds of thousands of Jews in Moslem lands are still being served by the JDC.

Since 1949, the ailing, the handicapped, and the aged among the immigrants to Israel have been assisted by Malben, an agency supported entirely by the JDC. The

annual $12 million absorbed by this continuing service—
nearly half the current expenditure of the JDC—reflects
the high proportion of broken minds and bodies among
the rescued.

Jonah worked for the JDC until the day he died in 1959.
Since then, the UJA has raised funds for current emer-
gencies at the same high annual rate as before, and the
JDC has administered aid through overseas headquarters
in Geneva and thirty field offices in Europe, Africa, and
the Near East. The determined spirit and solid organization of contributors and workers alike are Jonah's legacy
to American Jewry in the service of its own conscience.

· VIII ·

The Zionist Dilemma

ONE OF CHAIM WEIZMANN'S FIRST ACTS after being elected
President of Israel was to cite Jonah Bondi Wise for an
outstanding contribution toward the realization of Zionist
dreams and the establishment of the Jewish state. To say
that Jonah received the award with mixed emotions would
be an understatement.

The citation was unquestionably deserved. Jonah was
a friend to Israel and a friend to whom Israel owed much.
He had put his feelings about Zionism to one side during
a decade of extreme emergency and made common cause
with the Zionists on Zionist terms. That was a price ex-
acted by history for the rescue of hundreds of thousands of
Jewish lives. A small price under the circumstances, and
paid without hesitation. Certainly, to resettle Europe's
Jews where they could carry on a meaningful and purpose-
ful existence was an inescapable obligation. But, like many
others who clung to the classical principles of Reform
Judaism's founding fathers, Jonah never gave up his re-

171

servations about political Zionism. He was not pleased
by the establishment of a Jewish state, and felt distaste for
manifestations of Jewish chauvinism, American or Israeli.
America was his one and only Promised Land, and Judaism
was a religion, a church, and a body of ethics. If he did not
adhere to Zionism, Jonah was nonetheless unwilling to see
the Zionist question divide American Jews and cripple
their pursuit of common aims. History shows us, however,
that such matters are not easy to control. During the period
of struggle for the establishment of the Jewish state, the
dialogue between the dissenting minority of American Jews
and the Zionist-oriented majority was escalated from the
level of give-and-take to the level of bitter controversy.
Jonah played a somewhat ambivalent role in this drama.
His commitment to Jewish unity on the broadest possible
base and to support of Israel as a historic necessity were
stronger than his natural sympathies with the minority,
with whom he was at first aligned. He refused to pass over
from non-Zionism to active anti-Zionism, and eventually
found himself in the uncomfortable position of co-operating
with a group whose basic values he did not share and by-
passing an opposed group whose basic values he did share.
In so doing, he disturbed and disappointed not a few who
had counted—with reason—on his being one of their
number. His motives were misread and his position mis-
understood. It was said, for example, that he was a prisoner
of his office and associations in the UJA. It was also said
that his continued active and wholehearted promotion of
"illegal" Jewish immigration into Palestine after the cessa-
tion of hostilities in Europe departed from a position laid
down by Isaac Mayer Wise.

Whatever accusations might have been leveled against

Jonah with any justice at all, divergence from his father's views was never one of them. The elder Wise had conceived as his prime task the welding into a coherent American Jewish body of all the mutually suspicious elements from dozens of German and Polish regions and provinces. He had more than once acceded to the demands of entrenched Orthodoxy and patiently bided his time. As a young man in Europe, with foreknowledge of the consequences—jail, to which he went—he had disobeyed established authority in securing for his people some of the human rights denied them by the laws and police regulations of Austria-Hungary. Jonah knew exactly what Isaac Mayer Wise's thoughts had been about the settlement of Palestine by Jews from Europe. Furthermore, those thoughts had been expressed clearly enough in a communication printed in the *American Israelite*, April 17, 1863. Jonah kept many copies of it. A few paragraphs are excerpted below:

However indifferent one feels toward the land as a land, he cannot divest himself of a certain reverence and even awe that so many centuries inspire for the spots where our kings ruled, our bards sang, our prophets poured forth the glowing stream of inspired words, the daughters of Zion, the Sulamiths and the Deborahs lived, and the sons of Israel fought heroic battles against all mighty nations of antiquity. No intelligent mind can feel indifferent toward the land of liberty's birthplace, the cradle of civilization, the everlasting foundation to the temple of justice, the cornerstone in the superstructure of humanity—the land to which now the innumerable pilgrims of the three civilizing religions look with pious awe. It is mortifying to think that the sons of the Maccabees, the remains of the ancient race of God-inspired heroes now in that country, are in a wretched condition, and all our gifts lavished on them for centries, did not improve it.... They are Orientals indolent in every respect....

[We should] bring an industrious population into that country to develop its rich resources, and gain the rising generation of the present population to European and industrial habits. The "land which floweth with milk and honey" is as productive, the soil as rich, and the climate as congenial as in days of yore. Its geological wealth is immense, and its geographical position excellently adapted to trade and commerce, connected by steam navigation to all parts of Europe, Africa and the East Indies, having large and thickly populated countries in its immediate rear, who depend on the European market. In a few short years, telegraphs, railroads and commerce would follow the industrious colonist and rejuvenate the land. There is certainly nothing visionary in this prospect, nothing impracticable or the least unlikely....

We have no doubt many of our readers are favorably disposed toward this scheme, and we would therefore propose [that] a society to colonize Palestine should be organized in every congregation....

The angriest reaction to the formation of the Jewish state came from the American Council for Judaism. The Council was a voice for men who had once been Reform Judaism itself—until 1930 or so—and who thereafter had come to feel like so many displaced persons within their own religious family.

In 1937, the Reform rabbinate, convening at Columbus, Ohio, repudiated Isaac Mayer Wise's Pittsburgh platform of 1886, which had stated that "we consider ourselves no longer a nation but a religious community, and therefore expect neither a return to Palestine, nor a sacrificial worship under the sons of Aaron, nor the restoration of any of our laws concerning the Jewish state." Now, at this new convention, the Bar Mitzvah initiation ceremony was revived; Friday-Saturday Sabbath observance was explicitly made the cornerstone of the liturgy, thereby putting an end to an earlier drift toward Christian-style Sunday worship; and the authority of the Talmud was reinvoked. The Columbus resolution, in addition, went on to say that "in the rehabilitation of Palestine, the land hallowed by memories and hopes, we behold the promise of renewed life for many of our brethren. We affirm the obligation of all Jewry to aid in its upbuilding as a Jewish homeland, by endeavoring to make it not only a haven of refuge for the oppressed, but also a center of Jewish culture and spiritual life." The center of gravity of Reform Judaism, thus, was tipped in an Orthodox, ethnic, and Zionist direction.

Parenthetically, it might be added that Orthodox and Conservative Judaism were tipping toward Reform; the entire American Jewish community was being homogenized. This development was not to everyone's taste, particularly not to the polar groupings of ultra-Orthodox and classical Reform, both of whom were apprehensive for their identity.

At Columbus, Jonah took a firm stand against the resolution before the matter was brought to a vote. He accepted defeat with reasonable grace, however, bowing to the inevitable. For it was inevitable that Jews, as always when conscious of compelling dangers, would close their ranks and turn toward their ancestral past. In the unquiet year of 1937, the Nazis were throwing off all restraints in their systematic persecution of German Jews, and erupting Arab nationalism was in its second year of attacks in force against Jewish settlements in Palestine.

But Jonah was both disturbed and angry when, in February 1942, the Zionist contingent in the Central Conference of American Rabbis, violating a duly resolved

agreement of seven years' standing that no public stand
would be taken on controversial issues related to Zionism,
powered through a resolution calling for a "Jewish Legion."
The Legion would comprise volunteers from America and
other lands and take part in the war as a self-contained
military unit. In World War I, such a unit, almost entirely
Palestinian and East European in composition, had fought
the Turks and Germans in the Near East under the command of General Allenby.

The successful power play was an empty victory for
the Zionist-minded in the CCAR. Gripped by the passions
of the time, they were oblivious to the intensity of the
passions they were arousing in others. And to no realistic
purpose, for the direct appeal of a Jewish army to American
Jewish youths was absolutely nil. The majority of American
Jews who were Zionists were Zionists vicariously. They
were unreserved in their moral and financial support of
Jewish life in Palestine; this was their basic notion of
Zionism—and still is. It came under the heading of pious
works; the actual Zionist experience, particularly migration to Palestine, was something for those other Jews, un-
fortunates who needed help. "We have won the battle of
Pinsk versus Washington," Chaim Weizmann proclaimed in
1921, when Louis D. Brandeis was forced out of his position of leadership in the World Zionist Organization pre-
cisely because of this characteristic American Jewish attitude. But the rejoicing was premature. The enthusiasm
of some American Zionist leaders notwithstanding, Washington never took any cognizance of its defeat by Pinsk,
and the international Jewish Legion idea withered on
the vine for lack of nourishment. The only Jewish units in
World War II were Palestinian: a contingent of desert

troops in Egypt and North Africa, the Jewish Brigade in Italy and Germany both of which fought with distinction under British command—and the Haganah, the Palestinian Jewish community's own militia.

Resentments and frustrations that had been mounting for a decade and longer were triggered by the 1942 resolution into explosive release. The disruptive chain of events thereupon set into irreversible motion has seriously impaired the CCAR's capacity for united action over the past twenty-odd years.

The resolution was a bone in the throat to the unreconstructed Reform rabbis. In a fighting mood, they resolved to put their own interpretation of Reform Judaism on public record. On March 24, after six of them met in the office of Dr. Louis Wolsey of Philadelphia, invitations were wired to seventeen colleagues, Jonah among them, to come to Philadelphia to discuss what action should be taken over the resolution on the Jewish army. Jonah wired back his acceptance, and attended two meetings at which the main business was drafting an invitation to a caucus of the non-Zionists in the Reform rabbinate. When he saw the temper of his fellow committeemen, he voiced his own concern for the future of the Central Conference of American Rabbis and the Union of American Hebrew Congregations, two institutions that meant more to him than the issue that had brought the group together. No longer sure that he wanted a caucus at all, he asked for moderation in the statements to be put forward and urged that a search be made for a modus vivendi with the leadership of the CCAR. When the motion to caucus was put to a vote and carried—unanimously—he proposed a quite discreet wording for the letter of invitation. Jonah's

language was found a little too discreet, and Dr. Samuel
Goldenson of New York suggested adding that "the failure
to emphasize the universalistic elements of Jewish life
and thought" (a reference to growing Orthodox coloration)
and the "growing emphasis upon the racial and nationalistic aspect of Jewish thought" would have "an adverse
effect." The meeting was adjourned with the understanding
that both Jonah's wording and Goldenson's would be
taken into account.

The final invitation was prepared in accordance with
the sense of the meeting, but Jonah still did not like it.
He wrote Wolsey rather grumpily to that effect. Wolsey,
surprised, regretfully removed Jonah's name from the list
of sponsors—it was then Jonah's turn to be surprised—but
asked him to write a paper on postwar problems and to
appear on the program as a speaker on that topic. In
later correspondence he made it clear that he expected
Jonah to discuss alternatives to settlement in Palestine as
a solution to the needs of refugees. Jonah was too swamped
to prepare a paper, but agreed to speak. His name was
added to the invitation, and the caucus was set for June
1 and 2 at the Hotel Chelsea, Atlantic City. Invitations
signed by 24 non-Zionist rabbis were to be sent to a
selected list of 160 others.

Jonah need not have been apprehensive—if, indeed,
he was—that the call for a caucus would irrevocably an-
tagonize the more ethnocentered and Zionist-inclined
Reform rabbis. The officers of the CCAR circularized the
membership over the impending caucus. Although the
Zionist reaction was sharp—in some instances immoderate-
ly so—the men who ran the organization were not ready
to do battle. On the contrary, they rushed to smooth things

over, offering far-reaching concessions to their dissident colleagues. On May 11, the president of the CCAR, Dr. James Heller (who was also a top executive of the UJA), and Dr. Solomon Freehof of Pittsburgh met with Wolsey and Goldenson. The discussion was completely amicable. Heller put forward the view that the Atlantic City caucus, if held, would be interpreted quite generally as a secession, with disastrous results to the morale of American Jewry. He offered, in return for the cancellation of the caucus, to call the entire membership of the CCAR to a special meeting at which he would recommend the rescinding of the resolution on the Jewish Legion and the passage of a by-law that would make neutrality on Zionist issues an unbreakable rule of the CCAR. The CCAR would be committed to economic and cultural reconstruction of Palestine, but to nothing political.

Wolsey and Goldenson agreed to poll the signers of the caucus invitation. They did so immediately, recommending that Heller's offer be accepted and the caucus called off. They had won.

But the caucus was not called off. In just a few weeks, the movement of protest had acquired such momentum that the signatories were now incapable of accepting a truce that, basically, returned the situation to the *status quo ante*. If they were not to have their day in court, they wanted at least some confession of error by the other side. The vote on the Jewish Legion resolution would have to be expunged from the minutes of the February meeting of the CCAR. This demand was conveyed to Heller, who would not agree to it. In his report to the Reform rabbinate immediately thereafter, however, he admitted that he "may have been in error in not declaring the Army resolution out of order."

The caucus was held as planned. Jonah spoke, but there is no record of what he said. Wolsey gave the keynote address, beginning it with an account of the first six-man discussion in Philadelphia. It had been the consensus, he said, "that the Conference had through the years been so infiltrated with a nationalistic ideology as to change the thought and content and purpose of Reform Judaism. It was their unanimous conclusion that unless Reform Judaism was brought back to its original moorings and emphasis laid again upon the prophetic and universal ideas of Reform, then the movement which had achieved so much for the spiritual life of the occidental Jews was either to become something other than what its founders and their disciples intended it to be, or it was to be transformed into something which was its very reverse, or be annihilated altogether." The preacher of the sermon at the February convention, he complained, had accused the pioneer reformers of being overzealous to modernize Judaism, overeager to conform to recent thought rather than to tradition. He finished with: "Here we shall say whether....as some have asserted, Zionism is equivalent to the Jewish religion [or] whether the desire to create a Jewish state is a token of defeatism in religion and lack of confidence in the universal moral mission of Judaism....whether the nationalistic movement is counter to every thought and emotion of Jewish history; whether retreat to a nationalistic ghetto is a surrender of the great universal messages of Jewish prophet and sage; whether the imposition of a secular gospel—sometimes by outright coercion—is a part of American and Jewish democracy; whether we should yield our sacred Jewish traditions to a movement which is completely and deliberately non-religious and secular; in a word, whether we should consent to the destruction of our faith."

The classical Reform rabbis, thus, made their thoughts and feelings plain. When the angry speeches were over, a position paper was prepared that was a masterpiece of restraint; Jonah was the chief draftsman. Ninety-five Reform rabbis signed it, and it was sent out to the 500 members of the CCAR. The key paragraph read as follows:

Realizing how dear Palestine is to the Jewish soul, and how important Palestinian rehabilitation is towards relieving the pressing problems of our distressed people, we stand ready to render unstinted aid to our brethren in their economic, cultural and spiritual endeavors in that country. But in the light of our universalistic interpretation of Jewish history and destiny, and also because of our concern for the welfare and status of the Jewish people living in other parts of the world, we are unable to subscribe to or support the political emphasis now paramount in the Zionist program. We cannot but believe that Jewish nationalism tends to confuse our fellowmen about our place and function in society and also diverts our own attention from our historic role to live as a religious community wherever we may dwell. Such a spiritual role is especially voiced by Reform Judaism in its emphasis upon the eternal prophetic principles of life and thought, principles through which alone Judaism and the Jew can hope to endure and bear witness to the universal God.

So far, the controversy had stayed within the boundaries of the Reform rabbinate. Would it go beyond? Wolsey and his original group had wished from the first to give public notice that not all American Jews were Zionists. (A person less engaged would have concluded that Americans as a whole did not care very much, and noted that, among those who did care, more approved of Zionism than disapproved.) It was now proposed to release the non-Zionist position paper to the Jewish and national press, and, perhaps, to buy advertising space for it in the *New York Times*. Jonah, from the first, had wished to confine the dialogue to the Reform community as represented by its congregations and their rabbis, and still wished to do so. Non-Zionism had no organized base in the other branches of Judaism, except for the isolated splinter group of the persistently medieval ultra-Orthodox, to whom the redemption of Israel in the land of Zion was the province of the still-to-come Messiah and not to be undertaken by unsanctified mundane hands. It seemed to Jonah that the group's goal of halting the erosion of classical Reform ideas would in no way be furthered by public pronouncements and the spread of conflict.

In August, the statement was released to the press (over Jonah's objections), and in the next two months it received considerable exposure in news columns and editorial pages. The thrusts and pressures of the vast majority of the American Jewish population upon a nonconforming but strong and respected minority had produced a predictable counterthrust. The controversy was no longer a family quarrel within the CCAR.

"Traitors!" screamed the small body of religious Zionists. Other Jewish organizations also reacted adversely.

At this point, the rest of the American rabbinate might have been well advised to let the incident go by. Psychologically, however, it was impossible for them to do so; and the controversy now moved into a much larger sphere.

In November, 733 rabbis from all three major branches of the Jewish faith, 199 from the CCAR included, posted a full-page advertisement in the *New York Times* denying substance to the objections raised in the non-Zionist pronouncement and pointing out the minority status of the signatories even within Reform itself. In defending Zionism and rebuking their unruly colleagues, the 733 unwittingly gave the Atlantic City statement wider dissemination that it had achieved on its own.

Meanwhile, interest in the resistance movement of the non-Zionist rabbis had been stirred among like-minded Jewish laymen. In the East, wealthy laymen came forward to offer financial support. In the Midwest, there was a development of lay-rabbinical chapters. The leaders of the movement were encouraged by these signs to look toward a more broadly representative organization, lay as well as rabbinical in composition, national in scope, and with an active program of lectures and publications. It does not appear that they had determined upon a new organization when mustering their original protest: a caucus was one thing and a rabbinical organization outside the parent organization of the CCAR was another. Their intentions hardened when they caught sight of what might be a real opportunity to stem the tide of change in Reform Judaism. Certainly, the decision to establish an extramural organization came rather suddenly. A meeting with prominent laymen was agreed upon on November 23 and scheduled for the afternoon of December 5 in New York. It was held as planned. On the following morning, December 6, the *Times* announced that a new Jewish group was being formed, to be called "The American Council for Judaism." Rabbi Wolsey, in stating its aims, specified opposition to "a Jewish state, a Jewish flag or a Jewish army," but interest in "the development of Palestine as a refuge for persecuted Jews."

In six weeks, Jonah was to advocate the disbanding of

the organization at whose birth he had assisted, and, in seven, to leave it. He was the first of a rather long procession.

After the announcement that the American Council for Judaism had been formed, Heller asked for another meeting with its rabbinical principals. The meeting was held in Baltimore on January 5, 1943, with seventeen Zionist, non-Zionist, and neutral Reform rabbis present. Heller made a three-point proposal. The first point: that the Council agree to dissolve. The second: that the next convention of the CCAR adopt a by-law providing that, thenceforward, no official stand would be taken on questions of Zionist principles and that individual members would be left to think and act on such questions as seemed best to them; a qualifying clause would permit the CCAR to act on the physical, cultural, and religious rehabilitation of Palestine. The third: that conversations be initiated between representatives of the Zionist Organization and the erstwhile American Council for Judaism to find a common ground on Palestine and to work out methods for future co-operation.

The non-Zionist committee had its own meeting in Jonah's study. After twelve hours of discussion, it concluded that the conduct and attitudes of the non-Zionist rabbis were and had been unassailable, and that if the ACJ were to liquidate, "the laymen would lose faith in the rabbinate" and "in consequence...faith in religion." In addition, the new organization and the religious principles for which it stood had a bright future, for "thousands of laymen" were "anxiously awaiting the opportunity to join the ACJ." The committee voted "firmly and enthusiastically" not to liquidate. There was one dissenting vote: Jonah's.

Jonah was now thoroughly exasperated with his associates in the Council. They were anxious to use his name but loath to accept his judgment. For nearly a year, he had played one tune and been forced to dance to another. They had scrapped a chance to have more influence in the Jewish world, he thought, in order to follow a will-o'-the-wisp; intoxicated by an illusory hope of building a powerful mass movement, they were risking damage to three institutions that were as his father and his mother—the Central Conference of American Rabbis, the American Union of Hebrew Congregations, and Hebrew Union College. His own indispensable role in raising funds for refugees might suffer were he to remain with the new organization. He had intended none of these consequences in going to that initial meeting in Philadelphia ten months before. This was the end of the line.

"Dear Colleague," he began his reply to the circular in which the 95 rabbis who had signed the Atlantic City statement were asked to ratify the decision to continue. Until then his letters to Wolsey had opened, less formally, with "Dear Lou." Having thus coldly given evidence of his displeasure, he wrote that he was heartily in favor of accepting Heller's offer and disbanding the ACJ. He went on to say that, even though he was interested in the problem that the ACJ proposed to study, he would not commit his personal reputation to an organization that made serious mistakes every time it issued a statement.

The wounds inflicted upon the body of American Jewry by the emergence of the dissentient American Council for Judaism proved nothing worse than a light bruise or two.

The necessary conditions under which a deep schism might possibly have been feared were actually realized— the turmoil over Jewish migration to Palestine in 1946 and

1947, the fiery birth of Israel in 1948, a great American
Jewish wave of enthusiasm for the new nation and identifi-
cation with its struggles. But there was no schism. The ACJ
freely—and most heatedly—voiced its opposition to what
went on, and some of its members as individuals (the
organization made no official pronouncement) went on
strike against contributing new funds to the United Jewish
Appeal. Instead (for it would have been unthinkable to
refuse aid to Jews searching for a land in which to live),
machinery was set up to assist migrants who wished to go
elsewhere than Israel. Within the CCAR, the quarrel of
1942–1943 was not repeated. Nor did support of religious
institutions and community organizations dip significantly.
There was, thus, no schism; secession had never been intended by the anti-Zionists (as the Council could fairly be
called after 1948). "Morris!" cried Stephen S. Wise upon
meeting Rabbi Lazaron of the ACJ in Central Park, "When
are you returning to your people?" "I never left my people," Lazaron replied crossly.

The independent republic of Israel did not assume the
form for which Jonah had hoped. He had envisaged a postwar Palestine in which Jews, Christians, and Moslems
would share equally in an American-style pluralistic society
and state—a "nation of nations," as his favorite poet, Walt
Whitman, had bragged of the United States of America.
What he found when he actually visited Israel was quite
different and rather puzzling.

In September 1950, Jonah and Morris Troper, a veteran
JDC executive, attended a meeting of the European executive council of the JDC at its Paris headquarters in Rue
Saint-Dominique. There, the stupendous efforts and the
achievements of the previous year were reviewed and pro-

posals for 1951 brought forward. From Paris, the two men flew to Israel to taste the fruits of their labor over two crucial decades.

In Israel, Jonah was given the reception of a prince and entertained repeatedly with as much lavishness as the prevailing austerity allowed. This, as usual, he endured. He took pleasure, however, in exploring biblical sites and historic monuments that he had known all his life from books and pictures. "Israel," he wrote his children on his return to Paris, "is a most impressive but also most puzzling little land. But there is much one must take on credit or faith." He also wrote, "Met B. Balaban of movies in Tel Aviv. Matter of fact, it beats Lakewood, with a little better English and more smoking on Shabbat."

Like most visitors to Israel, Jonah was deeply impressed by the vitality and spirit of the people as they engaged in the "upbuilding" of their country. The UJA and the JDC had given the ingathered exiles much more than rescue and first aid. They had provided, both in Europe and in Israel, massive support for culture, education, and job training, so that, as soon as possible, immigrants could resume normal life. In and of themselves, however, the people of Israel were doing far more than this. Rather than perpetuating a piece of Central Europe set down in a corner of Asia, they were creating something new and rather exciting to recompense the world for the loss of one of its civilizations. To observe this happy consequence of his work gave Jonah, despite his puzzlement, deep satisfaction and a sense of fulfillment.

After landing in New York, he devoted his first sermon at Central Synagogue—on Veterans Day, November 11— to a strong plea for support of Israel, saying:

The Commonwealth of Israel was established by an over-whelming majority of the United Nations. This happened a little over two years ago.

The population of the new state was approximately one million, roughly divided half and half between the Arabs and Jews. With the abrupt withdrawal of the British mandatory power the new state was confronted with and solved the problem of the reorganization of public services and civil and police establishments. It immediately became involved in a bitter war. The Arab population was almost entirely hostile and proceeded to take up arms to fight the new state from within while it was being attacked on all sides from without. The new state had no military organization other than one which had been carried on almost entirely in secret under the continual disarming and harassing program of the British police. The nation sprang to arms and by a miracle of courage defeated its enemies from within and not only repelled the invasion from without but compelled the evacuation of disputed territory which later proved of enormous value to the new state.

A Commonwealth a little over two years old had, under the most distressing circumstances, organized a new state which offers complete safety and security to its citizens and to all who visit it. It has been admitted as a sovereign state to the United Nations. It has organized its consular and diplomatic service in all the great capitals of the world. It has provided for the health of all its inhabitants and insured a steady supply of food, clothing and shelter to its own citizens and to those who have been brought to it as fugitives from lands of oppression on three great continents. It has taken in and almost entirely absorbed four hundred thousand and more immigrants. This would be equal to the United States' taking in seventy-five million immigrants in two years. It has refused admittance to no person who knocked at its doors as a refugee from persecution. All this in addition to waging a bitter war. It has a modern civil and economic program, and has taken its place in the United Nations as an independent power in the capitals of the world.

All this has been done in the face of a continued hostility on the part of its neighbors. Israel is in a state of war. It must main-

tain an army under great expense. It must protect its borders, a
stone's throw from its important centers. It must maintain an
economy on a far higher level than any of its neighbors, since it
is responsible for this standard to the nations of the world who
look to it for social leadership.

To maintain these standards and to retain its place it is important that it receive adequate aid from the outside. This aid is
not a gift. It should not be considered such. It is the meeting of a
debt incurred by the world at large when the Israeli government
undertook to carry out the first mandate of the United Nations,
failing which the United Nations would have been compromised,
and when the State of Israel undertook to receive the hundreds of
thousands who came there and the hundreds of thousands who
will come there. Were it not for this refuge these immigrants
would have been a continuous burden upon the democratic nations of the world and a frightful indictment of the civilization
which we are trying to maintain.

As a rabbi of prominence, known to be both a non-
Zionist and a man who was high in the UJA and a bene-
factor of Israel, Jonah was often regarded as a contradictory
figure. And men of independent mind are always hard for
the public to understand, especially in the field of religion.
Jonah was no exception. He therefore received many
requests for clarification of his attitude on Israel and
Zionism.

In 1953, in answer to a man whom he had confirmed in
Portland thirty years before, he wrote:

I am not a Zionist. I am not a member of the American
Council for Judaism.

I mentioned with respect the Israeli Flag four or five years
ago. I have been a consistent worker for the help and reconstruction of our unfortunate Jews in Europe.

To a friend, in the same year, he wrote:

I suppose your request for some leadership in the Reform Movement could be answered if another Isaac Mayer Wise would appear on the scene. Unfortunately, his son does not have that kind of genius. However, I do not despair, as I believe the Reform Movement is going forward after its frightful setback because of enormous immigration and the impact of chauvinistic Zionism. These difficulties have in a sense been outlived and are now being met. Money is our need. Men like yourself should band together and find the money and then I think the leadership could be had. I know you do your best, but you cannot do it alone. You have to send out to all your friends and make them conscious of the great opportunity for help which lies within their financial aid.

If Jonah had unofficial harsh words for Zionism, he also, on at least one occasion, had them for the American Council for Judaism as well. It was characteristic of him that they were delivered when he felt that key institutions of Reform Judaism were being menaced—in this instance through a circularized suggestion that financial support be withheld in order to apply counterpressure against Zionist indoctrination. The offending circular came with a communication from a regional committeeman of the AJC, a man for whom he had personal affection and who had been one of his boys in Portland. Enclosed with the circular and the covering letter was a forthcoming article in the *Council News*. The article was a shocked and indignant account of a Leader Training Institute run by the youth division of the Union of American Hebrew Congregations at which a great effort had been made to create a completely Israeli atmosphere; the "Zionese" greeting "Shalom" had been used as the equivalent of "Hi" and the rabbis on the faculty had led 160 young men and women in the

Israeli songs "Artzah Alinu" and "Zum Gali Gali." Jonah's answering letter speaks for itself:

First let me wish you a very pleasant and happy year and then let me say that I sympathize with much that you have to say in your letter.

We are passing through a period of readjustment and facing difficulties due to a great many causes. The present generation of young and middle-aged rabbis has largely been recruited from families who have been and are Orthodox. They have come into the Reform movement with one leap from their Orthodox environment. One must take into account influences of this sort. I realize that the situation is not what we would wish it to be, but in view of the background history of the overwhelming majority of our ministry, I find that we have more than held our ground. You and I know that the emotional appeal of nationalistic Zionism arose from the frightful persecutions not only in 19th-century Russia, but also in the foul hatreds of Polish and German anti-Semites. I lived in Germany as a student and I know that there was never so brutally outspoken and degradingly vulgar an anti-Semite as the man on the street, the student in the university and the professor in the faculty. When you add to this the horrible picture of the massacre of the Jews by the Germans and their Balkan allies, you simply cannot look with complete fear on the resultant demand for a secure haven.

Let us be frank and acknowledge that 90 percent of the Jewish population of the United States today is either Orthodox in practice, in parental influence or in home customs. Orthodoxy and Zionism go together almost completely. The Conservative movement has inherited as one of the appeals to a large group the religious Zionism of Orthodoxy and its messianic enthusiasm as well as the contemporary, and I believe temporary, political and national phase of the movement. Zionism is one of the bulwarks of the Conservative movement. It would be as lost without it as the Christian Church would be without the salvation theory of the Crucifixion. Against this enormous stress the Reform movement has maintained a comparatively sane and forward-looking attitude. Its lines have been breached frequently but it has not seriously given in to the force of numbers and traditions. These things I trust you will bear in mind before we come to the specific matter to which you call my attention.

I deeply and bitterly resent the kind of letter sent out over the article, which, I believe, is unfair and biased.... The statement that...a Council organizer was not cordially received may be true, but I do not think it important.... He himself admits that one of the leaders whose work he criticized was a fugitive from the most brutal Nazi treatment. I would not have resented [his] attitude if he had not chosen to rush into print and if it had not been for the kind of letter which a member of the American Council for Judaism sent me as well as I suppose thousands of other persons. This letter by inference and innuendo attacks the Reform movement with a seeming intent to undermine it financially. This, I believe, comes under the heading of a dirty trick. I propose to support the Union despite its many mistakes, which I could recite to you by chapter and verse. I resent the action by the American Council for Judaism as completely unworthy of an organization, especially one pretending to concern itself with an enlightened Jewish program.

Letters and articles of this kind can be written about any movement. It is a species of Jewish McCarthyism which I consider contemptible. I shall be quite content if you show this letter to any persons interested in the matter.

I greatly value our continued friendship and also your keen interest in the problems of American Israel. I wish that you could see those problems from the standpoint of our past and present difficulties and our expectations of a victorious survival in the future. I firmly believe that we have held our lines with an understanding of our obligations as well as with a sincere concern for the problems and perplexities of our fellow Jews. Reform Judaism does not brush aside Orthodoxy and it cannot and would not as a decent religious movement condemn the inherited and deeply rooted emotions of our fellow Jews. It can only survive as a great, sympathetic force concerning itself with the highest ideals for our religion here and abroad. For that reason I hope the Union will remain active on the highest level for the great truths of Judaism as well as being tenderly concerned with the past and present sorrows of our people and with their deep emotional reactions to their deaths and wounds.

The quarter-century that has elapsed since the non-Zionist rabbis rose against the transformation of their religious institutions by Zionism and neo-Orthodoxy affords us today a better perspective than was available to them. The excitement over the emergence of Israel has subsided. Bonds of fraternal sympathy with the little new republic are as strong as ever. But, as many Council members fail to realize but the World Zionist Organization recognizes with dismay, American Jewry regards itself as flesh of American flesh; it feels itself in no sense to be in exile; it does not look upon Israel as a homeland. The movement that produced the Council can be seen more clearly now as a wave of nostalgia for the religious institutions and customs into which the Council members were born.

There is little likelihood that Reform Judaism of the classic pattern will return in quite its original form. But, as Jonah somehow felt in his bones, its mid-twentieth-century changes did not presage the return to traditional Orthodoxy feared by the men who clung so frantically to classical Reform. American neo-Orthodox or Conservative Judaism is hardly Judaism of the medieval type, other-worldly and oblivious to science; it is tied to the modern world. The rabbis of the Pale of Settlement would have thundered against it as an abomination unto the Lord. The march of Reform Judaism did not grind to a halt. It paused a moment, as it were, for consolidation with the other branches of Judaism as they finally drew abreast of Reform after their later start. The present generation of Jewish youth gives promise—disconcerting, no doubt, to the generation of rabbis whose entry into the house of Reform brought a renewal of traditional coloration—that the march toward untraditional religious forms is being renewed. In any case, it is hardly likely that Judaism will fail to be affected by the religious crisis of our time, as evidenced by the ecumenical movement in Catholicism and the "God is dead" movement in Protestantism. But the shape of tomorrow's Judaism cannot now be foreseen.

The Last Years

A T THE END OF WORLD WAR II, in 1945, Jonah Wise was
preparing for the five-year nonstop effort that would
raise $700 million for the UJA. He was also mulling over
plans for commemoration of Central Synagogue's centennial anniversary, which would take place in 1946 and be
celebrated by the Union of American Hebrew Congregations as well as by the synagogue itself. If he also took note
of the fact that 1946 would mark still another turning
point—he would then be 65 years old and eligible to retire
—he gave no outward sign.

He was not ready to retire. He had little talent for being
a mere spectator, much appetite for work and strenuous
recreation, and his vigor was almost undiminished. His
legs and feet troubled him on occasion, but neither so much
nor so often as to keep him from the Metropolis golf course
almost every Sunday afternoon. He was more inclined than
formerly to devote time to solitary pleasures. The pleasant
Tudor house that he had rented every summer for several

years was now up for sale. Encompassed by woodlots and
approached by a narrow back road that was little more
than tire tracks gouged out of bumpy terrain, it was rural-
seeming in spite of its location in suburban Hartsdale.
Jonah loved it, therefore, and purchased it as a retreat
where he could dig in the ground and come and go as he
pleased any month of the year. He fixed up a workshop in
the cellar; when the weather outside was too harsh for
gardening or golf, alarming sounds of hammering and
sawing would issue from it by the hour. No one, absolutely
no one, was permitted to enter upon pain of his extreme
displeasure. His family, rather feelingly, referred to the
cellar as the "bear pit."

On Veterans Day, November 11, 1946, Central Synagogue's centennial was commemorated jointly with the
centennial of Isaac Mayer Wise's arrival in America. The
hymn that followed the processional was "Let There Be
Light," written by Isaac Mayer Wise himself. The ceremonies were cosponsored by the UAHC; and every Reform
temple in Manhattan took part. The month of November
that year was set aside by UAHC as the "American Jewish
Cavalcade," a time for the rekindling of religious spirit and
the advancement of liberal Judaism. Jonah dedicated the
November broadcasts of the *Message of Israel* to the Cavalcade, with Dr. Maurice N. Eisendrath, director of UAHC,
as guest speaker. Central's neighbors, Christ Church
Methodist and Central Presbyterian Church, kindly
changed the sequence of union Thanksgivings so that the
1946 tripartite service could be held in Central as one of
the centennial constellation of events.

Observance of the centennial continued until the end of
the year. In December, Bloch's entire *Sacred Service* was

performed, with Lechner as soloist assisted by Lazar Weiner and an augmented choir, and a public forum on religion in America was conducted in the main auditorium of the synagogue house. The forum speakers, in addition to Jonah, were Dorothy Thompson, newspaperwoman and author, T.V. Smith, political philosopher from the University of Chicago, and Mrs. Harper Sibley, president of the United Council of Church Women. Both of these events were broadcast over WQXR, the radio station of the *New York Times*. The last event on the jubilee calendar was a dinner and dance at the Waldorf-Astoria attended by 475 persons.

Coincident with the centennial were two announcements: the first that the 75-year-old interior of the synagogue house would be renewed, the second that friends of Jonah had commissioned his portrait, which was to be painted by Joseph Margulies and presented to the synagogue, whose community center was already graced by a life-size marble portrait bust of Isaac Mayer Wise. James Rosenberg gave a kickoff dinner for the $300,000 fund-raising drive to finance the renewal of the synagogue house.

Jonah sat for the centennial portrait uncomplainingly. It was duly finished and, on March 20, 1947, at a short ceremony, the presentation was made by Rudolf Neuberger and Herbert Schwarz, president of the congregation.

The portrait shows us Jonah B. Wise seated and wearing the robes with which he had been invested in 1935 as a Doctor of Hebrew Laws of Hebrew Union College; in his hands he holds an open copy of Isaac M. Wise's *Reminiscences*, with a small picture of the author on the cover. Jonah's face at 66 looks out at us soberly, the eyes beneath the close-cropped graying hair steady behind their tortoiseshell glasses. The expression is calm—controlled rather

than serene—and the mouth is in a firm line. The smooth
contours and sensitive features of his youth have given way
to the bolder planes and sharply jutting nose and chin of
more advanced age, and the undisguised idealism of forty
years before has become a blend of skepticism and guarded
hope. This latter-day face—slightly more seamed in actuality than the somewhat indulgent brush of the artist
shows it—has seen civilization thoroughly disgraced, and is
aware that civilization may very well disgrace itself further. It is a handsome face and a face of unmistakable
decency. It does its owner credit, for (according to Abraham Lincoln, who understandably gave much thought to
such matters), even though we cannot hold men responsible for their faces before they are forty, after they are
forty we must.

The renewal of the synagogue interior took two years,
and in March 1949 the building was rededicated. At the
ceremonies, Jonah took for his text the story of the rededication of the Temple from *Second Kings*. The musical
program was the same as at the laying of the cornerstone
in 1870, when Isaac Mayer Wise had been the principal
speaker. Among the speakers at the rededication in 1949
was the State Department official Charles P. Taft, who
recalled that his father, the late President William Howard
Taft, had been a friend and neighbor of Isaac Mayer Wise
in Cincinnati. At a special convocation, the Jewish Theological Seminary, the center for rabbinical training of the
Conservative branch of American Judaism, now awarded
Jonah the honorary degree of Doctor of Hebrew Letters in
recognition of outstanding contributions to Judaism and
Jewish life. The citation was made by Rabbi Robert Gordis,
the biblical scholar. Jonah was now three times a doctor,

having received an honorary Litt. D. from New York University in 1932.

The year 1949 saw his first real vacation in more than a decade. On June 23, Helen and Jonah Wise had been married forty years. They marked the occasion by an evening spent in the company of their children and a few family friends, and, soon after, sailed for Europe, where they toured Italy, Switzerland, and France.

It was the last such time they would have together. Less than a year later, Helen Wise died quite suddenly. At an afternoon meeting of the Sisterhood, she slumped forward in her seat just as David Seligson, Central's assistant rabbi in the years following World War II, had begun to deliver the concluding benediction. Seligson was by her side instantly, and helped revive her. Seemingly not unwell, she was taken to a hospital in an ambulance. That night, May 8, 1950, her heart stopped beating. She and Jonah had been married for 41 years. A private funeral, with Rabbi Louis I. Newman presiding, was held at the house in Hartsdale. All the flowers were from Jonah's own garden, and he picked them himself.

The home over which Helen Wise had presided had been the strong rock from which Jonah had descended each morning to face a rough and wayward world. The life was now gone out of the city apartment where they had lived so long, and Jonah transplanted himself and his possessions to the house in Hartsdale, where he felt less exposed and lonely. A manservant took care of his needs, and he shuttled daily between Hartsdale and Central Synagogue.

The thoughts of many were now turned in Jonah's direction. A stained-glass window commemorating Helen

Wise was installed in Central Synagogue and dedicated in November 1950. At the beginning of the following year, plans were forwarded for a public demonstration of esteem for Jonah himself. The committee formed for the purpose was composed of persons who had been associated with him in religious, philanthropic, and civic life on both working and policy-making levels. The name of Senator Herbert Lehman headed the list of committee members. Other members included Nathan Ohrbach, chairman of the committee, Emanuel Steindler, then president of Central Synagogue, and Alfred Bachrach, Paul Baerwald, Isidor Coons, Mrs. David M. Levy, Edwin F. Rosenberg, William Rosenwald, Edward M. M. Warburg, and Edmund Waterman. It was their thought to make a notable affair of the dinner to be tendered Jonah in recognition of his seventieth birthday and his 25th year as rabbi of Central Synagogue, and to create a substantial fund that would ensure him comfort and security for the rest of his life.

The dinner was indeed a notable affair. It was held at the Waldorf-Astoria on Sunday, February 25, and attended by 500 persons from all parts of the United States. The speeches were a great outpouring of affection and praise. Among the speakers were his old friends from the Protestant ministry, Dr. Ralph W. Sockman of Christ Church, Methodist, and Dr. Theodore C. Spears of Central Presbyterian Church; David Sarnoff, board chairman of RCA; Rabbi Maurice N. Eisendrath, president of the Union of American Hebrew Congregations; Dr. Nelson Glueck, president of Hebrew Union College-Jewish Institute of Religion; and C. Ludwig Baumann, merchant and philanthropist.

Sockman, saluting Jonah as a "friend, a colleague, a

great soul, and a man of God," said that he had "extended his ministry to the ends of the earth. His comradeship with other faiths has been matched by his statesmanship in world-wide philanthropy." Speers also took note of Jonah's interfaith efforts, remarking that New York's Protestant ministers were daily conscious of his "friendship, his standard of work as God's servant, his standard of values as a man and a public servant, and his outreach of compassion and kindliness." Eisendrath called Jonah a "one-man civil-defense agency and a public-relations ambassador from the Jewish community to our neighbors." Sarnoff paid tribute to his pioneer work in religious broadcasting. Finally Jonah, before responding with a concluding speech, was presented with a testimonial scroll and a sum of money to be used as he saw fit.

Jonah's earnings had always been respectable and his expenditures modest. He had a few investments, and Ochs had left him a small bequest of shares in the *New York Times*. But he had educated three children, and his personal donations to the various organizations that he served in the capacity of executive or trustee had always been considerable, especially to Hebrew Union College and the Union of American Hebrew Congregations. He had felt a certain obligation to pay his own way in order to work on a basis of absolute freedom and equality with associates who were often men of great wealth—his own contributions, of course, being in proportion to his own resources—and had taken pride in doing it. Thus, the total of his financial resources did not come to very much, and, though he had no great personal need of money, he was pleased to be in a position to build an estate. He still had no intention of retiring, for his work was his life.

Honors and recognition continued to pour in upon Jonah, who was now called upon frequently to appear over television and radio in the capacity of elder statesman of Judaism. His completion of fifty years in the rabbinate was marked on December 17, 1954, by a special Friday evening service in which forty civic leaders and clergymen of all faiths marched in a procession in his honor. A citation from Hebrew Union College-Jewish Institute of Religion hailed him as "one of the most contributive and distinguished leaders of American Judaism of this generation." The *New York Times* had already taken note of the occasion with an article by Jonah himself in the *Times Magazine* of December 12. In the article Jonah once again stressed interfaith co-operation. "We are living in a period of religious resurgence," he declared, "a period in which people, more than ever, are turning toward some form of belief which can sustain their courage and their faith in their fellow humans. And there has been a drawing together of different religious groups, an increase of understanding and sympathy of one sect for another."

Public testimonials had lost a good deal of their freshness for him by the time his 75th birthday came around two years later. He chose to celebrate it privately and in his own way, taking his three children and five grandchildren on a midweek sentimental journey to Cincinnati. The party of twelve piled into a rented station wagon, which he drove around the city, taking them to Hexter's Hotel, his birthplace, the old Isaac M. Wise Temple on Plum Street, and the Isaac M. Wise farm in suburban College Hill.

Jonah changed greatly in the years that followed his wife's death. He became increasingly more withdrawn, confining the circle of people whom he saw to his family and a few friends and associates. He devoted much time to his grandchildren, in whose company he took comfort and pleasure, and often brought them along when he called on the old friends whom he still visited. But, even though he went about his affairs with courage and resolution, he could no longer maintain his life on the even keel of his married years. He had been more dependent on his wife than anyone had known except himself. Without her, his decisiveness hardened into brusqueness and impatience. He found humanity woefully unredeemed. To those who were still close to him, his dissatisfaction was plainly with himself, although others were often made to feel its brunt. After expressing discouragement with men in general, he would follow by saying, "Really, I am sick and tired of looking at this face." Listening to the playback of a tape for the Armed Forces Radio Service, he would shake his head and remark to a protesting Lechner, "I am certainly no speaker. And I have absolutely no command of the English language." But, standing in the pulpit, he was once more in his element. As he set about his customary task of giving courage to his hearers, his pessimism fell away, and he would end on a positive note.

It was thirty miles from Hartsdale to Central Synagogue and thirty miles back, some of it over rough terrain and much of it through bruising traffic. He liked driving, but the long trip became a burden, especially on weekends, when Sabbath services at Central on Friday night and Saturday morning were followed by the *Message of Israel* service on Sunday morning. The High Holy Day round of services was particularly exhausting. Of necessity, he rented a room at the Hotel Adams on Fifth Avenue at 86th Street, staying there when he was too weary to go back to

Westchester or faced an especially heavy schedule in the city. He also leaned rather heavily on the assistance of David Seligson. Although he trusted Seligson completely and had much affection for him, he sometimes felt left out of the picture when he had left the planning of services completely in Seligson's hands. On such occasions, he might change the planned and posted order of service at almost the last minute—the musical offerings included, so that soloist, organist, and choir would have to rush around and get new music, sometimes music for which they did not feel properly rehearsed. Minor inconvenience to other people did not trouble Jonah too much, especially if he told himself that he was keeping them on their toes. He was considerate in large ways. His sense of fairness would not allow him to keep Seligson in the capacity of assistant rabbi, and he arranged for the younger man's elevation. From 1954 until Jonah's death early in 1959, Central had two rabbis of equal rank.

David Seligson came to Central as assistant rabbi in 1945 after a three-year army chaplaincy in the Burma-India theater, and a short stay at Port Chester, N.Y. Previously, he had served for five years as rabbi in Birmingham, England, whither he had been invited by Sir Claude G. Montefiore, British exponent of Liberal Judaism. Seligson was a scholar rather than an executive—of his two doctoral degrees from Hebrew Union College one was earned, not honorary—a Hebraist, and a convinced Zionist, with strongly traditional leanings. Jonah, who was so different in background, personality, and attitude, had no difficulty in assessing Seligson's capacity to serve Central well and maintain its reputation for a strong congregation and ministry. Upon arriving at Central, the younger man immediately performed in a manner that made him Jonah's first choice as his successor.

During the last six months of his life, Jonah needed all his courage. Never a good sleeper, he now hardly slept at all, and was tortured by arthritic pains in his feet. The constant driving to and from Hartsdale was altogether too much for him. He grew visibly weaker. Isaac Stern, a trustee of Central, an enthusiastic supporter of the *Message of Israel*, and one of Jonah's few intimates, saw him almost daily. He begged Jonah to retire, and Jonah reluctantly agreed to do so after Stern would return from a forthcoming journey and make necessary arrangements. Stern never saw him again.

During those last days, Jonah gave much thought to the *Book of Job*, the poetic drama of the doubts engendered in a religious mind by unmerited suffering; Archibald MacLeish's *J.B.* was then running on Broadway. Jonah read from *Job* to his congregation at the next-to-last service at which he presided. At the rehearsal before the broadcast of the *Message of Israel* of the following week, he discussed the play *J.B.* with Lechner. "The ending was added," he said. "It doesn't really belong. The real ending was despair. Why do the just suffer?" Then, "Lechner, I would like you to be taken care of." And, to the chauffeur, "Will you please be good enough to take Mr. Lechner safely home?"

At the broadcast itself, the following Sunday morning, he paused halfway through his sermon. There was a long silence before he resumed. He then stumbled to the Ark, in order to recite the *Kaddish*, and once more faltered in the middle. After the program, he doggedly attended a funeral, at which he collapsed. His brother-in-law, Dr. James

Rosenfeld of Portland, who was in New York at the time, examined him and immediately sent him to Doctors Hospital, where he lost consciousness and died, after an illness of a week, on February 1, 1959. He would have been 78 years old three weeks later.

Among the thousands of letters and telegrams to the Wise family and Central Synagogue, a few words by Judge Ben Shapiro of Bridgeport, Connecticut, stand out for their concentrated expression of loss to the entire Jewish world. "A giant tree," Shapiro wrote, "has fallen in Israel."

*   *   *

JONAH BONDI WISE carried forward an important tradition in American Judaism, and was himself a living symbol of it. He was an ambassador of the air waves. He was a savior of a multitude. By any standard, he had a distinguished life.

Unlike most distinguished lives, his was achieved without penalty to the rest of the world. Jonah Wise never fanned a disagreement into open conflict nor sought to destroy a rival, never bullied a subordinate nor patronized a person whom he was doing a service. His tongue, if sharp, was not lethal. His lapses from grace were such as giving voice to an imprudent quip or forgetting some detail about a man he was burying, and only emphasized his membership in the tenaciously imperfect human race. He did not jeopardize his manhood by regarding himself as a different order of being above the rest of mankind—the besetting sin of the great and powerful. To be a rabbi he saw as the highest of callings, and to be a Jew and an American the rarest of privileges; but he saw himself first as a man among men. His common humanity was precious to him, and he protected it by respect for the humanity of others. He built upon it to shape a career that he summed up himself—as Rabbi David Seligson touchingly noted in a tribute to his predecessor shortly after his death—when he stood before his congregation for almost the last time and read from the 29th chapter of the *Book of Job*:

The princes refrained talking, and laid their hand on their mouth.
The nobles held their peace, and their tongue cleaved to the roof of their mouth.
When the ear heard me, then it blessed me; and when the eye saw me, it gave witness to me:
Because I delivered the poor that cried, and the fatherless, and him that had none to help him.
The blessing of him that was ready to perish came upon me: and I caused the widow's heart to sing for joy.
I put on righteousness, and it clothed me; my judgment was as a robe and a diadem.
I was eyes to the blind, and feet was I to the lame.
I was a father to the poor: and the cause which I knew not I searched out.
And I brake the jaws of the wicked, and plucked the spoil out of his teeth.

Acknowledgments

THE WRITING OF THIS BOOK was made possible by the generous co-operation of the following persons: Hon. Jonah J. Goldstein, I. Edwin Goldwasser, Rabbi Samuel Gordon, Rabbi Hugo Hahn, Elsa Wise Hertzberg, Joan Wise Kaufman, Moses Leavitt, Frederick Lechner, Dr. Hubert Mann, Regina Wise May, William Rosenwald, Dr. Joseph Schwartz, Herbert Schwarz, Rabbi David J. Seligson, Rev. Ralph W. Sockman, Rev. Theodore Speers, Anna Bird Stewart, Edward M. M. Warburg, Dr. Leon Watters, Rabbi J. J. Weinstein, and David J. Wise. Dr. Samuel Sandmel and Dr. Jacob J. Marcus extended to me the facilities of the American Jewish Archives and supplied me with a number of documents. I am particularly indebted to Isidor Coons and to Rabbi Max Merritt, both of whom not only provided me with much information that would otherwise have been unobtainable but went to considerable effort to present it in coherent and easily usable form.

S. C.

Index

209